D1165092

He Touched Them

In the still air, the music lies unheard.
In the rough marble, beauty hides unseen:
To make the music and the beauty needs
The master's touch, the sculptor's chisel keen.

Great Master, touch us with Thy skillful hand;
Let not the music that is in us die!
Great Sculptor, hew and polish us; nor let
Hidden and lost Thy form within us lie!

Horatius Bonar

IDEALS PUBLICATIONS INCORPORATED
NASHVILLE, TENNESSEE

Editor's Note

What little we know of Jesus' brief ministry comes from the Gospels, which repeatedly tell of Jesus healing the sick and saving the lost. Countless writers and artists have been moved by these stories of Jesus' love and power. In poetry, fiction, essays, sermons, drawings, and paintings, these men and women have given faces and personalities to the disparate group of people who knew Jesus firsthand and whose lives were transformed by His presence. In the pages that follow, we have gathered a selection of these writings, paintings, and drawings, along with Scripture passages and modern photographs of the Holy Land, in the hope that by studying how Jesus touched the lives of those who knew Him, we will come to a deeper understanding of Jesus the Christ.

ACKNOWLEDGMENTS

Ideals Publications Incorporated has made every effort to trace the ownership of all copyrighted material. Thanks are due to the following authors, publishers, and agents for permission to use the material indicated:

Buechner, Frederick: "What Good Can Come From Nazareth?" from *Peculiar Treasures: A Biblical Who's Who.* Copyright © 1979 by Frederick Buechner. Reprinted by permission of HarperCollins Publishers, Inc.

Gibran, Kahlil: "Mary Magdalene" from *Jesus the Son of Man.* Used by permission of The National Committee of Gibran, copyright © all rights reserved. Copyright © 1928 by Kahlil Gibran and renewed © 1956 by Administrators CTA of Kahlil Gibran Estate and Mary G. Gibran. Reprinted by permission of Alfred A. Knopf Inc.

Hinkson, Katherine Tynan: "The Ten Lepers." Reproduced with the permission of the executors of Katherine Tynan and Pamela Hinkson estates, 1996.

Johnson, James Weldon: "The Prodigal Son" from *God's Trombones.* Copyright © 1927 The Viking Press, Inc., renewed © 1955 by Grace Nail Johnson. Used by permission of Viking Penguin, a division of Penguin Books USA Inc.

Marshall, Peter: "Disciples in Clay" and "The Touch of Faith" from *Mr. Jones, Meet the Master,* copyright © 1949, 1950. Reprinted with permission of Fleming H. Revell, a division of Baker Book House Company, Grand Rapids, Michigan.

Mauriac, François: "Come, Follow Me"; "The Samaritan Woman"; and "The Rich Young Man" from *Life of Jesus,* translated by Julie Kernan. Copyright © 1937 by Longmans, Green and Co. Reprinted by permission of Librairie E. Flammarion.

Pasternak, Boris: "Miracle" from *Doctor Zhivago.* First published in Great Britain by Collins and Harvill 1958. Copyright © 1958 Giangiacomo Feltrinelli Editore, in the translation by Manya Harari and Max Hayward. Copyright © 1958 William Collins and Co., Ltd. Reproduced by permission of The Harvill Press. Copyright © 1958 by Pantheon Books, Inc. Reprinted by permission of Pantheon Books, a division of Random House, Inc.

Payne, Robert: "On the Road to Emmaus" from *The Lord Jesus.* Reprinted by permission of JCA Literary Agency, copyright © 1964 by Robert Payne.

Poteat, Edwin McNeill: "Barabbas Speaks" from *Over the Sea, The Sky.* Copyright © 1945 by Harper & Brothers, renewed © 1973 by William H. Poteat, Elizabeth P. Terry and Haley G. Poteat. Reprinted by permission of HarperCollins Publishers, Inc.

Sheen, Fulton J.: "A Parable for Public Officials" from *Thoughts for Daily Living.* Copyright © 1956 by Doubleday, a division of Bantam Doubleday Dell Publishing Group. Used by permission of Doubleday, a division of Bantam Doubleday Dell Publishing Group, Inc.

Studdert-Kennedy, G. A.: "Gambler" from *Quotable Poems, Volume 2* by Thomas Curtis Clark. Copyright © 1928 by Harper & Brothers, renewed © 1956 by Hazel P. Davis Clark. Reprinted by permission of HarperCollins Publishers, Inc.

Turnbull, Agnes Sligh: "The Miracle of Cana" from *Far Above Rubies.* Reprinted with permission of Fleming H. Revell, a division of Baker Book House Company, Grand Rapids, Michigan.

The drawings on pages 18 through 29 were created by Spanish artist
Jose Fuentes de Salamanca.

Publisher, Patricia A. Pingry; Editor, Nancy J. Skarmeas; Copy Editor, Michelle Prater Burke; Book Designer, Tina Wells Davenport

Color Film Separations by Precision Color Graphics, New Berlin, Wisconsin

Published by Ideals Publications Incorporated
535 Metroplex Drive
Nashville, Tennessee 37211

Copyright © 1997 by Ideals Publications Incorporated
All rights reserved.

No part of this publication may be reproduced or transmitted in any form or by any means,
electronic or mechanical, including photocopy, recording, or any information storage and retrieval system,
without permission in writing from the publisher.

Printed and bound in the U.S.A by R.R. Donnelley & Sons, Willard, Ohio

ISBN 0-8249-4083-0

First Edition
10 8 6 4 2   3 5 7 9

Contents

Jesus Led Them

During the era in which Jesus lived, it was not uncommon for men to apprentice themselves to religious leaders or scholars and devote their entire lives to learning a religious faith and its practice. At first glance then, the band of twelve men who followed Jesus might appear as simply ordinary, especially for this part of the world. Upon closer examination, however, there were remarkable differences between Jesus and His disciples and other religious leaders, not only of His time, but of all time.

First of all, not one of the twelve disciples chose Jesus; He chose them. They did not seek Him out; He came to them. And He chose His followers carefully. Not one of the disciples was a career holy man. Not one came from the religious community. Instead, Jesus chose an unlikely band that included fishermen, a political activist, and even a tax collector.

These disciples were so transformed by Jesus' presence in their lives that after only three years of following their Master, they were equipped to carry His message to every corner of the world.

It is this ability of Jesus—to turn ordinary, uneducated, simple men into the dynamic leaders each would become—that is explored in the following pages. The original twelve were only the first of the countless throngs that, through the centuries, would leave all and follow the Master.

Disciples in Clay

*If any man
serve me,
let him follow me;
and where I am,
there shall also
my servant be:
if any man serve
me, him will my
Father honour.
John 12:26*

uppose you had been on . . . a committee nineteen hundred years ago, to inquire into the qualifications of those who sought to become disciples of Jesus. . . . Here comes the first candidate. He has just come up from the beach. His fishing boat, drawn up on the pebbled shore has worn seats, patched sails, and the high rudder that is characteristic of Galilean fishing craft.

As you can judge from his appearance, he has just entered middle age. But he is already bald, and the fringes of hair that remain are already gray. His hands are rough and calloused. His fingers are strong. He smells of fish! He is an uncouth person—not at all refined, or cultured, or educated. Blustering, blundering, clumsy, impulsive, he does not strike us as being material for the ministry. Then, too, his age is against him. Maybe he is too old. Why, he is forty if he is a day. Does not the ministry demand young men? . . . We cannot ignore his age—and this man's age is against him. His ideas will be very hard to change. He will be stubborn. Set in his ways. He is a rough man, and he has lived a rough life. When provoked, he is liable to burst into profanity, and his vocabulary is lurid. Can you imagine this big fisherman as a disciple of Jesus? He would not be your choice, would he? No, we'd better send Simon back to his nets.

The next candidates are brothers; they come in together. They, too, like Simon Peter, are fishermen. They come from the same village, from the same colony of rough, strong men who work with their hands for a living. But you are not going to hold that against them, are you? Let no social snobbishness sway your judgment. Remember the Lord Himself was a carpenter. There is no shame in manual labor, and would it not be to a preacher's advantage to know what it is to do manual labor? Would it not be excellent preparation for the ministry? These two men are looking at you. Their eyes are steady, accustomed to far distances. They are good weather prophets. A glance at the sky and a look at the lake, and they can tell you what is brewing. They know the signs of the sudden squalls that whistle through the mountain passes and come screaming down to make the water dangerous. They, too, have strong hands and nimble fingers. They make quite a team, these brothers. They operate a boat in partnership, and they are very successful. In fact, it is a mystery to their competitors how they always manage to find the fish, always catch more than the other boats, and how they manage to get better prices for their catch. This naturally does not increase their popularity among the fishermen.

But it is chiefly their attitude that irritates the others. They are not modest men. They are boastful, and through cupped hands they like to shout taunts to the other fishermen hauling on their nets. They have earned for themselves the nickname "the sons of thunder," because they are always rumbling about something. The way they feel, they have little patience with people who cross them, and they would be inclined to call

On the preceding pages, flowers bloom on a shoreline of the Sea of Galilee. In northern Palestine, the Jordan River flows into a deep basin, bordered on both sides by mountains, to create the Sea of Galilee, a heart-shaped lake twelve miles long and seven miles wide. Jesus' home village of Nazareth lies in the rocky hills to the west of the Sea of Galilee, and He performed His first miracle in another small Galilean mountain village called Cana. After turning water into wine at Cana, Jesus traveled east to the Sea of Galilee; and it was in the cities, villages, and countryside surrounding this lake that word of the great teacher Jesus of Nazareth first began to spread.

down fire from heaven to burn them up. Get rid of objectors! That's their motto. They are ambitious men, and if the stories are true that are whispered about them, they have been brought up to believe that if you want anything in life—grab it. Their mother had taught them that to get on in the world you have to push. They would want to be in the chief places. They think they belong in front. If they became disciples of Jesus, they would naturally want to be His chief lieutenants—one on His right hand and the other on His left. If we took time to hear all the testimony from people who know them, our verdict would be unanimous that James and John would simply not do.

So let us pass on to the next candidate. There is a wild gleam in his eyes—and no wonder. He is a leader of the Underground. He seems to be of the fanatical type, impatient and nervous. See—he cannot keep his hands still—his fingers clench and unclench. They itch to reach up and haul down the hated pennants of Rome that hang in desecration from the walls of old Jerusalem. His blood fairly boils when he is forced, by some clanking legionnaire, to make way on the pavement and step into the gutter. He dreams of the day when the Kingdom shall be restored to Israel, and the promise of the sacred writings, that when the Messiah comes He shall restore the Kingdom, is his meat and drink. His eyes dance at the thought of the Messiah, at the head of a liberating army, driving the hated Romans into the sea. Yes, from the hill country they would come, and from the cellars of the Holy City they would rise up to bring back the glories of David and of Solomon. He wants, more than life itself, to be a part of that glorious campaign. But this young man might be too dangerous. He is highly inflammable material. He is likely to become violent, and his impatience will burn him up. He is a great risk—a very great risk. We could not take a chance on Judas. We dare not.

Notice how the ladies greet this next candidate. He will have their vote right away. We are all drawn to him, and the men, however grudgingly, have to admit that he is handsome. He walks with an easy grace. There is nothing effeminate about him, but he is gentle, refined, every inch a gentleman. Endowed with all the social graces, who could possibly say a word against him? His eyes are like limpid pools. His smile melts your heart. But when he starts the day, it is not to take up the tools of his trade, for he has none. It is not to yoke the oxen to work in the fields, for he never soils his hands. It is to wander off to day-dream. He is a Ferdinand sort of man. He likes to smell the flowers. He is an introvert—a dreamer. But don't you know that the work of the Kingdom demands extroverts—men who are interested in other people? Don't you realize that it is not castles in the sky we pray for—but the coming of the Kingdom of God upon this earth? We have to pray for it—and work for it, too. No, Nathaniel is a good man, everybody agrees, but he is simply not the type we need.

We are not doing very well in selecting disciples, are we? But think of the material we have to choose from. Well, what about this fellow? He, too, is a fisherman. Let's not hold that against him. If you are not a tradesman, or a farmer cultivating a bit of land, dressing some fruit trees or tending grapes, if you have no sheep or goats, there isn't much else for you to

And Jesus, walking by the sea of Galilee, saw two brethren, Simon called Peter, and Andrew his brother, casting a net into the sea: for they were fishers. And he saith unto them, Follow me, and I will make you fishers of men. And they straightway left their nets, and followed him.
Matthew 4:18–20

And going on from thence, he saw other two brethren, James the son of Zebedee, and John his brother, in a ship with Zebedee their father, mending their nets; and he called them. And they immediately left the ship and their father, and followed him.

Matthew 4:21, 22

The disciples who answered Jesus' call left everything to travel by His side. Their mission was not only to learn Jesus' message and carry it to the people after He was gone, but to form a community of believers living the life which Jesus preached. They renounced their worldly goods and lived pure and rustic lives among the poor, the sick, and the outcasts of the world. In a painting opposite by Leslie Benson, Jesus calls two fishermen to follow Him.

do but fish. For people have to eat, and fish is the best money crop in this part of the country. This man might have it in him to be a disciple. He is not impulsive by any means. He will not be swept off his feet. He is very cautious, slow to convince. He must have been born in some little Palestinian "Missouri." You have to show him. He demands proof for everything. He'll take nothing on faith. Now, this twist of mind and character will always slow up the work of any group to which he might belong. He will be like the rusty little tramp steamer in the convoy. He'll slow down the others to his own wheezy seven or eight knots. In fact, he has only two speeds, dead slow and stop. Can you imagine him as a member of the apostolic band? Always advocating delay. "This is not the time" will be his theme song. "Let's wait and see," will be his advice. But the Kingdom is a venture of faith—not of doubt. It is a matter of perception—not of proof. How could Thomas possibly fit into that picture?

Now if we were Jews living at the time the disciples were originally chosen, we would boo or hiss as this next candidate enters, for he is a Quisling. He has sold out to the army of occupation and is collecting taxes for the Roman government. . . . Tax collectors are seldom the most popular men in any community, and this fellow is a racketeer to boot. He has devised his own particular racket and it is making him many enemies and making him rich as well. But that's not all. He has a mind like an adding machine. He has been counting money all his life. Money and evidences of wealth alone impress him. That's bad enough, but there's worse to come. He is a genealogist. He is one of those men whose passion is family trees. He will bore you with long recitals of the best families—where they came from, whom they married, how many children they had, and whom they married and so on . . . and on. Can you imagine a Quisling as a friend of Jesus, a statistician walking with the Carpenter from Nazareth, a man who had made a god of money? No Levi, or Matthew if you like, must be rejected.

What about this fellow Andrew? Does anyone know about him? I have heard it said that he has no personality—whatever that means. I know that he is Peter's brother, but I know of no good reason why he should be chosen.

There are others still waiting—Bartholomew, Thaddeus, Philip and another James, and a man called Simon from Canaan. They are all interested in becoming disciples, but I know of no particular reason why they should. We would not vote for any of them. . . .

I feel sure you would not argue with me if I suggested that these men had more influence on the course of human history than any other dozen men who ever lived. Each man was different. . . .

Had you and I been members of any investigating committee we would have rejected every one of them. Yet Jesus chose them.

PETER MARSHALL
FROM MR. JONES, MEET THE MASTER

On the Road

And they brought young children to him, that he should touch them: and his disciples rebuked those that brought them. But when Jesus saw it, he was much displeased, and said unto them, Suffer the little children to come unto me, and forbid them not: for of such is the kingdom of God. Verily I say unto you, Whosoever shall not receive the kingdom of God as a little child, he shall not enter therein. And he took them up in his arms, put his hands upon them, and blessed them.

Mark 10:13–16

As depicted in this painting by George Hinke in which Jesus is surrounded by young boys and girls and their mothers, Christ often reached out to little children. In their innocence and humility, He found a perfect model to teach us how to approach God. The lesson was clear: God was a loving and all-forgiving father.

For road-mates and companions he chose twelve,
All, like himself, of homeliest degree,
All toilers with their hands for daily bread,
Who, at his word, left all and followed him.
He told them of The Kingdom and its laws,
And fired their souls with zeal for it and him.
He taught a new sweet simple rule of Right
'Twixt man and God, and so 'twixt man and man—

That men should first love God and serve Him well.
Then love and serve their neighbours as themselves.
They loved him for his gentle manliness,
His forthright speech, his wondrous winning ways,
His wisdom, and his perfect fearlessness,
And for that something more they found in him
As in no other.

For through the mortal the immortal shone—
A radiant light which burned so bright within
That nought could hide it. Every word and look,
And a sweet graciousness in all he did,
Proclaimed him something measurelessly more
Than earth had ever seen in man before,
And with him virtue went and holy power. . . .

Through all the land he journeyed, telling forth
The gracious message of God's love for man—
That God's great heart was very sore for man,
Was hungering and thirsting after man,
As one whose dearly loved have gone astray,
As one whose children have deserted him.

The people heard him gladly, flocking round
To catch his words, still more to see his deeds,
The men all hopeful, and the women touched
By this new message and the messenger;
And everywhere the children drew to him
And found in him a sweet new comradeship.

Strange was his teaching, stranger still his deeds—
He healed the sick and gave the blind their sight,
With his own hands cleansed lepers of their sores,
And raised the dead—all in the name of God,
And for the love God's great heart held for them.

JOHN OXENHAM
1861–1941

Political Leaders of Israel

"And it came to pass in those days, that there went out a decree from Caesar Augustus, that all the world should be taxed. . . . And Joseph also went up from Galilee . . . unto the city of David, which is called Bethlehem" (Luke 2:1, 4a). Bethlehem of Judea was conquered by the Romans in 63 B.C. and became part of the massive Roman Empire, which stretched from the northwest corner of Europe to Egypt and from Mauritania to the Black Sea. More than fifty million inhabitants lived under the relatively stable rule of Augustus Caesar, the first Roman emperor. Augustus organized this vast region and brought peace to the diverse peoples, a peace which would prove crucial to the spread of Christianity since Jesus' disciples were able to travel unimpeded to the far corners of the Roman Empire.

Under the Romans, the Jews could practice their religion and were granted some special rights; but the Empire was still pagan, and conflicts with the monotheistic Jews were frequent and often violent. The Jews resented the influences of a foreign culture and the taxes Rome imposed. Roman occupation brought improvements in daily life, such as better roads, increased trade, and beautiful architecture; but as long as the Romans remained, the ancient land of Palestine remained in bondage.

"Where is he that is born King of the Jews? for we have seen his star in the east, and are come to worship him" (Matthew 2:2). This question, asked in Jerusalem by the Magi, troubled no one more than Herod the Great, reigning king of the Jews. Herod ruled Judea from 37 to 4 B.C. (the year of Christ's birth) and was, at times, an effective, although irrational, leader. Under his rule, Judea prospered and built a magnificent array of palaces, parks, theaters, and fortresses. Herod's most ambitious project by far was the transformation of the five-hundred-year-old, decaying temple in Jerusalem into a magnificent house of worship.

Powerful as he was, however, Herod was also probably mentally ill. A half-Jew by birth, yet a Roman citizen as well, he imagined threats in every corner, even among his family. He had one of his wives, his mother-in-law, a brother-in-law, and three sons assassinated. By the time the Magi came to Jerusalem, Herod was so irrational that he decreed all male children in Judea under the age of two be killed; Jesus, however, was already in Egypt. Within three years, Herod the Great was dead and his kingdom divided among his three surviving sons.

Emperor Augustus Caesar, pictured above, then known as Octavian, came to power in Rome after the assassination of Julius Caesar in 44 B.C. He ruled first as a part of a triumvirate that included Mark Antony, but eventually came to hold sole power over the vast Roman Empire.

The Sanhedrin, whose name comes from the Greek *synedrion*, meaning counsel, was the highest ruling body of the Jewish people. Composed of priests, elders, and scribes of the Jewish synagogue, the Sanhedrin was presided over by one ruling high priest and controlled most of the day-to-day business of the Jewish courts of law. Historians are not certain as to the exact jurisdiction of the Sanhedrin; but they do know that in certain matters, court cases were taken to the Roman governor for sentencing, which is why Jesus was brought before Pontius Pilate.

The Sanhedrin convicted Jesus of blasphemy for His teachings; but when they delivered Him to Pilate, they told the Roman governor that Jesus was guilty of "perverting the nation, and forbidding to give tribute to Caesar." Led by the high priest Caiaphas and the former high priest, Annas, the Sanhedrin urged Pilate to sentence Jesus to death.

The Roman coins at left bear the image of Constantine the Great, the first Christian emperor of Rome, who reigned from A.D. 306 to 337. Constantine began the use of the cross as a symbol of Christianity when he had the Greek letters Chi and Rho engraved upon the shields of his soldiers; the two letters together form the shape of a cross.

The stone above bears the inscription legia x fretensis, *signifying the Roman legion that destroyed Jerusalem in A.D. 70.*

As Roman governor of Judea from A.D. 26 to 36, Pontius Pilate had judicial authority over the Jewish people and the power to impose sentences and enforce the law. His overriding concern was protecting his position among the political intrigue of Roman government, and his insensitivity to the religious beliefs and traditions of the Jews resulted in increased resentment and periodic uprisings. After one such riot, Pilate momentarily lost his political instincts and ordered a group of Samaritans executed. For this rash act, he was finally called back to Rome.

But Pontius Pilate will be forever known as the man who condemned Jesus to death. Pilate hesitated in his condemnation, probably because of political concerns with the Sanhedrin; but when he turned to the crowd, which was probably assembled by the Sanhedrin for political purposes, he threw the question of Jesus' fate to them. The mob, incited by the priests of the Sanhedrin, called for Jesus' death. Pilate, ever the politician, obliged and sentenced the Son of God to die.

At right are the remains of an architecturally graceful Roman aqueduct where Caesarea once stood. Built by King Herod in the first century B.C., Caesarea was a city with no Jewish roots and a distinctly Roman character. Pontius Pilate lived there, and the city was the headquarters for Roman soldiers sent to crush the Jewish revolt that began in A.D. 66.

Come, Follow Me

And it came to pass, that, as the people pressed upon him to hear the word of God, he stood by the lake of Gennesaret, And saw two ships standing by the lake: but the fishermen were gone out of them, and were washing their nets. And he entered into one of the ships, which was Simon's, and prayed him that he would thrust out a little from the land. And he sat down, and taught the people out of the ship.

Luke 5:1–3

One of the two was Andrew, the brother of Simon; the other was John, son of Zebedee. . . . What did Jesus do to keep them? "Jesus turning around and seeing that they followed him, saith to them, 'What seek ye?' They said to him, 'Rabbi . . . where abidest thou?' He saith to them, 'Come, and ye shall see.' They went therefore and saw where he abode, and they abode with him that day; it was about the tenth hour."

The text of the gospel narrative is as moving as any direct words of Christ. . . . That which passed between them at that first meeting, in the dawn of Bethany, was the secret of a more than human love, love inexpressible. Already the lighted fire was catching from tree to tree, from soul to soul. Andrew told his brother that he had found the Christ, and brought back to the desert with him Simon, who from that day forward Christ called Kephas.

The next day the conflagration spread, reached Philip, a native of Bethsaida, as were Andrew and Peter. The words and acts which attached him to Christ are not known to us. But the flame spread from Philip to Nathanael. This new tree did not take fire at once, for Nathanael was versed in the Scripture and protested that nothing good could come out of Nazareth. His friend answered simply: "Come and see."

Was it enough for each of these chosen souls to see Jesus in order to recognize him? No, Jesus gave each a sign; and the sign he gave Nathanael was the same he was soon to use to convince the woman of Samaria. "Whence dost thou know me?" Nathanael had asked in a distrustful tone. "Before Philip called thee, when thou wast under the fig tree, I saw thee." Nathanael at once replied: "Thou art the Son of God."

It matters little that the secret act which took place beneath the fig tree was never revealed. What Nathanael discovered was that the very depths of his being were known to this man; he felt himself open before him, as do the least of us today, kneeling for the avowal of our sins or with our faces turned toward the Host. During his mortal life Christ was prodigal of that sign which caused many a simple and unaffected being to fall with his face against the earth. He replied even to the most secret thoughts of the scribes and the Pharisees, but they, far from striking their breasts, saw therein but a ruse of Beelzebub. The faith of the humble Nathanael surprised Christ more than their incredulity, and we may imagine his smile as he said: "Because I said to thee, 'I saw thee under the fig tree,' thou believest. Greater things than these shalt thou see."

Perhaps when this encounter with Nathanael took place, Jesus had already left the desert, where during forty days he had fasted and suffered the attacks of the Prince of Evil. Going up to the Jordan by Archelais and Scythopolis, he had reached the Lake of Tiberias and Bethsaida, the native country of the disciples who had left John to follow him. Not that the hour of total abandon had as yet sounded for them. Their nets and their barques were still to hold them for a little while; they had had only the first call. . . .

Jesus with his followers went to Capharnaum, to the shores of the lake where Simon, Andrew, James and John found once more their boats and their nets. His grip on them loosened for a little while; they would never escape him again. We have read the story so often it seems simple to us that Jesus, passing along the shores of the lake and seeing his friends cast down their nets, had need of only the words, "Come, follow me and I will make you fishers of men," for them, without so much as a turn of the head, to leave all and follow him. However, it was not without his having given them a new sign of his power, chosen from among all those which might most surely strike these simple minds.

He had first borrowed their boat in order to escape the people who pressed too closely upon him. Simon had rowed out a little way, and Jesus, seated in the stern, spoke to the multitude grouped around the water's edge, to a multitude in which feeling ran high, for already there was great division of opinion concerning him. In Nazareth, in the synagogue (where like any other pious Jew he had the right to speak) his commentaries on the prophecies had irritated the people who had known him from his earliest years. To them the carpenter Yeshua was of little importance, despite the cures which were beginning to be laid at his door. Their irritation had reached its height when he had let them understand that the Gentiles would be preferred to them, and it was only by a miracle he had escaped their fury.

Now he no longer risked being alone: here he was in the boat with Simon and the sons of Zebedee. Since that day in Bethany, these boatmen knew that he saw into the secret life of each one of them; they had seen with their own eyes the miracle of Cana; Jesus had cured Simon's mother-in-law of fever. It remained for him to touch them in that which counted for most in their eyes: to catch as many fish as they wished—it was their job to know that was extremely difficult.

Indeed they had worked all that night without catching anything. And now Simon had to call James and John to his help to draw in the nets. The two boats were so full of fish they were almost sinking. Then Kephas fell to his knees. "Depart from me, for I am a sinful man, O Lord." Jesus' answer, like many of his words, contained a prophesy which we are still seeing fulfilled before our eyes: "Henceforth thou shalt catch men."

FRANÇOIS MAURIAC
FROM *LIFE OF JESUS*

Now when he had left speaking, he said unto Simon, Launch out into the deep, and let down your nets for a draught. And Simon answering said unto him, Master, we have toiled all the night, and have taken nothing: nevertheless at thy word I will let down the net. And when they had this done, they inclosed a great multitude of fishes: and their net brake. And they beckoned unto their partners, which were in the other ship, that they should come and help them. And they came, and filled both the ships, so that they began to sink. When Simon Peter saw it, he fell down at Jesus' knees, saying, Depart from me; for I am a sinful man, O Lord. For he was astonished, and all that were with him, at the draught of the fishes which they had taken: . . . And Jesus said unto Simon, Fear not; from henceforth thou shalt catch men.

Luke 5:4–10

*And he said unto another,
Follow me. But he said, Lord,
suffer me first to go and bury
my father. Jesus said unto
him, Let the dead bury their
dead: but go thou and preach
the kingdom of God. And
another also said, Lord, I will
follow thee; but let me first go
bid them farewell, which are
at home at my house. And
Jesus said unto him, No man,
having put his hand to the
plough, and looking back, is
fit for the kingdom of God.
After these things the Lord . . .
sent them two and two before
his face into every city and
place, whither he himself
would come.*
Luke 9:59–62; 10:1

Obedience

I said, "Let me walk in the fields."
He said, "No, walk in the town."
I said, "There are no flowers there."
He said, "No flowers, but a crown."

I said, "But the skies are black;
There is nothing but noise and din."
And He wept as he sent me back;
"There is more," He said; "There is sin."

I said, "But the air is thick,
And fogs are veiling the sun."
He answered, "Yet souls are sick,
And souls in the dark undone."

I said, "I shall miss the light,
And friends will miss me, they say."
He answered, "Choose tonight
If I am to miss you, or they."

I pleaded for time to be given.
He said, "Is it hard to decide?
It will not seem hard in heaven
To have followed the steps of your Guide."

I cast one look at the fields,
Then set my face to the town;
He said, "My child, do you yield?
Will you leave the flowers for the crown?"

Then into His hand went mine,
And into my heart came He;
And I walk in a light divine,
The path I had feared to see.

GEORGE MACDONALD
1824–1905

*Artist Richard Hook portrays
Jesus as the compassionate
friend and kind leader described
in biblical accounts.*

Peter

And Jesus, walking by the sea of Galilee, saw two brethren, Simon called Peter, and Andrew his brother, casting a net into the sea: for they were fishers. And he saith unto them, Follow me, and I will make you fishers of men. And they straightway left their nets, and followed him.
Matthew 4:18–20

Called from the shores of the Sea of Galilee, the fisherman Simon would become the leader among Jesus' apostles. Simon was emotional and impulsive, but he first recognized Jesus' divinity. When Jesus asked His disciples who they said that He was, Simon alone replied, "Thou art the Christ, the Son of the Living God." For this declaration of faith, Jesus renamed the apostle *Peter*—the Greek word for rock—and declared that it was Peter's belief upon which Christianity would be built (Matthew 16:18).

Yet those strong feelings that drew Peter to Jesus made for a tumultuous relationship with his beloved Lord. Peter's overwhelming love for Jesus prevented him from accepting Jesus' explanation of His upcoming death. As Jesus was arrested and led away, Peter bravely followed Him to the garden of the chief priests, only to lie under questions about Jesus of Nazareth. After these trials, or perhaps because of them, Peter gains strength.

After Jesus' resurrection, Peter dramatically became an articulate spokesman at Pentecost and went on to carry the gospel to Antioch, Asia Minor, and Rome. It was Peter who insisted Jesus' message was universal and open to all who confessed their faith; and it was Peter who first preached the gospel to the Gentiles.

According to tradition, Peter was martyred in Rome in A.D. 61. The story is told that Peter tried to flee the city when his arrest appeared imminent; but a vision of Jesus entering Rome to be crucified again, this time in Peter's place, convinced the disciple to return to his own death. Peter requested that he be crucified head down, as he felt unworthy to die in the same position as Jesus. To the end, Peter was guided by his emotional, yet passionate, devotion to his Christ.

John

And when his disciples James and John saw this, they said, Lord, wilt thou that we command fire to come down from heaven, and consume them, even as Elias did? But he turned, and rebuked them, and said, Ye know not what manner of spirit ye are of. For the Son of man is not come to destroy men's lives, but to save them.

Luke 9:54–56a

John, with his older brother James, was a fisherman on the Sea of Galilee; and he also became an apostle of Jesus. A member of the inner circle of disciples, John was perhaps the closest of all the apostles to Jesus. His life is an illustration of the power of Jesus to transform ordinary men.

Typical of Galilean fisherman of his day, John was rough and emotional with a violent temper. When Jesus and His disciples were going to Jerusalem, the Samaritans offended John and he became violently angry. His Master's calm rebuke reminded John that, in following Jesus, he had chosen the way of peace and love.

Traditional stories give us further information about John's life. It is generally believed that John was the "beloved disciple" to whom Jesus committed His mother's care as He was dying on the cross. Legend holds that John was faithful to this charge and remained in Jerusalem with Mary until her death. Then he traveled to Rome and suffered great persecution but remained true to the teachings of his Lord.

In later life, on the island of Patmos and in the town of Ephesus, legends emerge of John as a man of peace and quiet devotion. One legend is particularly telling—old and weak, John was still a beloved teacher in the church at Ephesus. He became almost too weak for speech and answered all questions with Jesus' admonition that we love one another. When questioned as to why he uttered only these words, John replied that love was the heart of Jesus' message. One of the "sons of thunder," who in his youth had been quick to anger, had come to believe in love above all else.

Andrew

One of his disciples, Andrew, Simon Peter's brother, saith unto him, There is a lad here, which hath five barley loaves, and two small fishes: but what are they among so many?
John 6:8, 9

Andrew brought the young boy with the loaves and fishes to Jesus in the same spirit of optimism that he had brought his brother, Simon, to meet the Lord, and that he would later bring the Greeks who searched for Jesus in Jerusalem. Andrew understood that Jesus would accept and make use of all who sought him in good faith.

A fisherman from the village of Bethsaida, Andrew, according to the Gospel of John, was a disciple of John the Baptist when he heard John acknowledge Jesus of Nazareth as the Lamb of God. From that moment until his death, Andrew was a devoted missionary for Jesus. The Gospels depict a quiet man—nearly always in the shadow of his brother—who happily accepted his often anonymous role.

In tradition Andrew emerges, after Jesus' ascension, as an active and devoted disciple. In Greece he converted several prominent citizens but angered the governor, who ordered Andrew arrested and crucified. Legend tells that Andrew requested an X-shaped cross. Like his brother Peter, Andrew felt himself unworthy of a death that mirrored that of Jesus. Andrew's death inspired many Greeks to faith in Christ.

Centuries after his death, Andrew's memory continues to inspire people. One legend tells of an eighth-century monk who had a vision that he was to take Andrew's remains to the west. The monk ended his journey in Scotland, where he founded St. Andrew's church. Soldiers from the area, fighting a battle against the English, reported that they saw and were guided by the cross of St. Andrew shining in the sky above the battlefield. Today, Andrew is the patron saint of Russia, Greece, and Scotland. The disciple who carried on his mission quietly and often in the shadows continues to represent Christ to the world.

Thomas

Thomas saith unto him, Lord, we know not whither thou goest; and how can we know the way? Jesus saith unto him, I am the way, the truth, and the life: no man cometh unto the Father, but by me.
John 14:5, 6

Thomas was a man of pessimism and doubt. It was he who continually questioned Jesus, he who was troubled by his inability to understand. In the Upper Room, Thomas resisted Jesus' prophecy of His fate; after the resurrection, Thomas withheld his belief until his eyes and hands confirmed what his ears had heard.

Doubt alone is not the story of Thomas. It is the answer Jesus provides, the resolution of Thomas's doubt, that is instructive. Jesus does not condemn Thomas for expressing doubts, which arise from a desire for more complete understanding, nor does He try to persuade. Jesus' answer is Himself. "I am the way," He tells Thomas in the Upper Room; and after the resurrection, He presents His body for Thomas's doubting hands to feel. Jesus' challenge to the doubter is to battle doubts with faith. Thomas exclaims to Jesus upon putting his fingers in the resurrected Lord's wounds: "My Lord and my God." Faith born in struggle emerges strong and pure.

One legend concerning Thomas, although its authenticity is questionable, nevertheless demonstrates the disciple's personality. After Christ's resurrection, Thomas was supposedly assigned the ministry of India by the group of disciples. Thomas refused to go, doubtful that he could carry Jesus' message to this foreign land. Jesus appeared to him in a vision, however, calmed his doubts, and convinced Thomas to go. The legend continued that, once in India, Thomas became a man of great and inspirational faith. True or not, the legend emphasizes the lesson of Thomas's life: doubt and pessimism in mankind are natural, but deep faith in Christ reveals that through God all things are possible.

Matthew

He went forth, and saw a publican, named Levi, sitting at the receipt of custom: and he said unto him, Follow me. And he left all, rose up, and followed him. And Levi made him a great feast in his own house: and there was a great company of publicans and of others that sat down with them. But their scribes and Pharisees murmured against his disciples, saying, Why do you eat and drink with publicans and sinners? And Jesus answering said unto them, They that are whole need not a physician; but they that are sick. I came not to call the righteous, but sinners to repentance.

Luke 5:27b—32

e know the publican Levi as the disciple Matthew, a tax collector from Capernaum who left his work to follow Jesus. In Jesus' time, there were few men more despised than those who collected the Roman taxes, since payment to Rome was against the Jews' religion that taught that only God deserved such tribute.

In addition to the religious concern, there was a more earthly reason to hate the tax collectors. They had a reputation for immorality and injustice: more often than not, they collected more money than was required and kept the difference. We don't know whether Levi was such a scurrilous man, but as a tax collector, he was indeed an unlikely disciple.

Yet once chosen, Matthew proved truly faithful and desired to spread the good word immediately. Evidence of his faith exists in the use he made of one of the tools of his former trade: his pen. Blessed with the skill of writing, Matthew left a record of the life and teachings of Jesus.

Although scholars dispute how much of the Book of Matthew in the Bible canon was actually written by the disciple, it is certain that Matthew wrote about Jesus and thus was instrumental in bringing countless people to Christianity. Jesus called Matthew to repentance. Matthew answered, and his life was transformed.

Judas Iscariot

Then one of the twelve, called Judas Iscariot, went unto the chief priests, And said unto them, What will ye give me, and I will deliver him unto you? And they covenanted with him for thirty pieces of silver. And from that time he sought opportunity to betray him.
Matthew 26:14-16

Judas Iscariot was the only one of the twelve apostles not from Galilee. Scholars believe that his name means Judas from Kerioth and that he hailed from a city by that name in Judea. Judas is the disciple who betrayed Jesus to the Roman authorities who arrested and eventually crucified Him.

Christians have debated Judas' motives for hundreds of years. One argument is that Judas lost faith in Jesus as the true Messiah and was greedy; another has Judas troubled by Jesus' association with sinners and questioning His leadership. Judas has also been portrayed as a man frustrated by Jesus' unwillingness to use force to assert His rule—perhaps Judas was a member of a radical group who wanted to overthrow Roman rule by violence. Perhaps he believed so strongly that Jesus was the Messiah who would lead the Jews to earthly freedom that he lost track of Jesus the Son of God who taught peace and love and repentance. Perhaps Jesus chose Judas, knowing he would betray Him, specifically so that the Scriptures might be fulfilled. The answers to these questions can never be known.

Accounts of Judas' downfall after the betrayal differ in their details. In the book of Matthew, Judas immediately hangs himself. In the Acts of the Apostles, Judas buys a burial field with the thirty pieces of silver then collapses and dies there. Whatever the circumstances, Judas could not live with the consequences of his act.

Judas is an example of a person who could never fully accept Jesus as Lord. Like the rich, young ruler, Judas could not relinquish his worldly life and commit himself to his Lord. When the time came to choose, he betrayed his Lord and lost his life in the process.

Philip

Philip saith unto him, Lord, shew us the Father, and it sufficeth us. Jesus saith unto him, Have I been so long time with you, and yet hast thou not known me, Philip? he that hath seen me hath seen the Father.

John 14:8, 9a

Philip, from Bethsaida on the north coast of the Sea of Galilee, was the first disciple to hear the simple command, "Follow me" (John 1:43) from Jesus; he answered the call and became a devoted missionary. Philip appears in the first three Gospels only in lists of the apostles. He comes to life, however, in the book of John.

Philip's first act after hearing Jesus' call was to find Nathanael and tell him the news that the Messiah, long promised by the prophets and by Moses, had come. Nathanael was skeptical; rather than argue with him, Philip simply urged Nathanael to go and see Jesus for himself.

Later, when a group of Greeks approached Philip in Jerusalem, hoping to be taken to meet Jesus, the disciple sought out Andrew and together they took the Greeks to Jesus, certain that the Greeks too would be overcome by faith in the presence of the Master.

A legend of Philip proves that the faith born in his first encounter with Christ remained his guiding light. Philip had been preaching in Hierapolis, and his church was composed of a large group of Christians. When sentenced to die by the leaders of Hierapolis for his preaching, Philip did not just quietly accept his fate. At his execution, he called upon the ground to open up and swallow the thousands who looked upon him. At that, Jesus appeared to Philip and rebuked him. Calmed by the vision of the risen Christ, Philip accepted death and requested only that his body be wrapped in papyrus rather than linen, which was used to wrap the body of Christ.

In this final act, Philip recalled the faith born out of his first step as a disciple, when he heard the two words that would ever after guide his life: "follow me."

imon, known both as Simon the Canaanite and Simon the Zealot, is mentioned only four times in the New Testament. In the Gospels of Matthew, Mark, and Luke, his name appears only as part of a list of apostles; in the passage at left, from Acts, we learn only that Simon remained with the disciples after Jesus' ascension.

What little we know about the man Simon comes from his designation as a Zealot. The Zealots were a radical Jewish party that emerged after the death of Herod the Great, when Judea fell under the rule of a Roman governor. Zealots were devoted to strict adherence to Jewish law, which included the belief that God alone was their ruler. Their resistance to Roman rule was absolute and violent; Zealots were prepared to sacrifice their own lives and the lives of any who cooperated with the Roman government. For a Zealot to become a disciple of Christ is then truly amazing. To follow Jesus, Simon had to lay down his weapons, quiet his anger, and pledge his belief in the sacrificial love of Jesus as the source of salvation.

Simon

And when they were come in, they went up into an upper room, where abode both Peter, and James, and John, and Andrew, Philip, and Thomas, Bartholomew, and Matthew, James the son of Alphaeus, and Simon Zelotes, and Judas the brother of James. These all continued with one accord in prayer and supplication, with the women, and Mary the mother of Jesus, and with his brethren.
Acts 1:13, 14

James

And going on from thence, he saw other two brethren, James the son of Zebedee, and John his brother, in a ship with Zebedee their father, mending their nets; and he called them. And they immediately left the ship and their father, and followed him.
Matthew 4:21, 22

James of Zebedee answered the call of Jesus without doubt or hesitation; he left behind his fishing boat, his nets, and his father to become a disciple along with his brother John. Very little is known of James. Along with John and Peter, he was part of Jesus' inner circle of disciples, these three witnessed Jesus' transfiguration on the mountaintop, and Jesus selected them to accompany Him as He prayed in the Garden of Gethsemane.

Jesus' characterization of James and his brother as "sons of thunder" implied that James had a fiery spirit. We know that he was outspoken and ambitious from the Gospel of Mark. Mark relates the story of a request made of Jesus by James and John, who asked that they be given places by His side in His kingdom. Jesus answered, "Ye know not what ye ask. Can ye drink of the cup that I drink of? and be baptized with the baptism that I am baptized with?" (Mark 10:38). Without hesitation, James joined John in answering, "We can." James was bold enough to ask for a place by Jesus' side and confident enough to profess himself worthy.

In A.D. 44, James proved his faith as strong as his words. In that year he became the first of the apostles to die for his faith when Herod Agrippa ordered him beheaded. Facing death, James did not waver from his strong faith. Tradition tells that on the way to his execution, James converted his jailer, who professed his own belief in Jesus as Christ and was executed alongside the apostle.

Bartholomew

And it came to pass in those days, that he went out into a mountain to pray, and continued all night in prayer to God. And when it was day, he called unto him his disciples: and of them he chose twelve, whom also he named apostles; Simon (whom he also named Peter,) and Andrew his brother, James and John, Philip and Bartholomew, Matthew and Thomas, James the son of Alphaeus, and Simon called Zelotes, and Judas the brother of James, and Judas Iscariot.

Luke 6:12–16

Little is known of Bartholomew; he appears by name alone in the Gospels of Matthew, Mark, and Luke. And in John, when the disciples are mentioned, the name Bartholomew seems to be replaced with that of Nathanael. Many scholars believe that Bartholomew and Nathanael are the same man. If this is the case, then the Gospel of John offers our only glimpse at the character of this silent disciple.

In John 1:45–51, Philip told Nathanael that Jesus of Nazareth was the Messiah of whom the prophets spoke. Nathanael doubted, yet followed Philip out of curiosity, perhaps, to see the man called Jesus.

In His presence, Nathanael's doubts dissolved to be replaced by faith in Jesus as the Messiah. No great miracle precipitated this belief, simply Jesus' words of recognition: He already knew Nathanael. He saw into Nathanael's heart, and Nathanael instantly acknowledged Him as Lord: "Rabbi, thou art the son of God: thou art the King of Israel." Nathanael (Bartholomew), a thoughtful man who waited to make up his own mind about Jesus of Nazareth, was moved to discipleship by the simple presence of the Son of God.

James, Son of Alphaeus

And he ordained twelve, that they should be with him, and that he might send them forth to preach, And to have power to heal sicknesses, and to cast out devils: And Simon he surnamed Peter; and James the son of Zebedee, and John the brother of James, . . . And Andrew, and Philip, and Bartholomew, and Matthew, and Thomas, and James the son of Alphaeus, and Thaddaeus, and Simon the Canaanite, And Judas Iscariot.

Mark 3:14–19a

Less is known about James of Alphaeus than of any of Jesus' twelve apostles. James's name appears four times in lists of the apostles, and that is all. Even legends are few.

It is believed that James preached in Persia and was eventually crucified for his faith. Some scholars have argued that James was the brother of Matthew, who is also identified as a son of Alphaeus. Others believe that James was a Zealot like Simon, for his name always appears joined with that of Simon the Zealot. Given these two assumptions, James would have been in an interesting position: a brother of a tax collector—a Roman collaborator—and a member of a group that believed all such men as Jesus should be put to death for their "betrayal of God." Only in discipleship and with the peaceful message of Jesus could such an inner and personal conflict have been resolved.

There is additional conjecture that James son of Alphaeus is the same man as James the Less, whose mother—a woman called Mary—is present at Christ's death upon the cross (Mark 15). James of Alphaeus, at last, remains a true mystery: a man of faith and devotion whose life was given to Jesus.

Judas, Brother of James

The apostle named Judas, not Iscariot, in the passage from John, is identified as Thaddeus in the Gospels of Matthew and Mark, and as Judas, the brother of James, in Luke and Acts. Scholars, for the most part, agree that the references in these five books refer to one man.

The passage at left is the only biblical evidence we have as to the character of this disciple. The question Judas put to Jesus indicates that Judas had some desire that Jesus make use of His great power to forcibly take command of the kingdom of the Jews. Jesus used the opportunity to remind Judas that His was a rule of love, not of violence, and it was not faith surrendered to force that would gain salvation for man, but only by following Christ.

One legend exists of Thaddeus. After Christ's resurrection, Thaddeus traveled to the city of Edessa to preach the gospel and to fulfill a promise made by Jesus to that city's king who, sight unseen, had accepted Jesus as the Son of God. Jesus had promised him that for his faith, the king would be healed. If Thaddeus and Judas are one, then his selection as the disciple to heal the King of Edessa is ironic. The disciple who urged Jesus to show His power to the world comes face to face with a man whose faith required no such display of worldly sign.

Judas saith unto him, not Iscariot, Lord, how is it that thou wilt manifest thyself unto us, and not unto the world? Jesus answered and said unto him, If a man love me, he will keep my words: and my Father will love him, and we will come unto him, and make our abode with him.

John 14:22, 23

Now Philip was of Bethsaida,
the city of Andrew and Peter.
Philip findeth Nathanael,
and saith unto him, We have
found him, of whom Moses in
the law, and the prophets,
did write, Jesus of Nazareth,
the son of Joseph. And
Nathanael said unto him,
Can there any good thing
come out of Nazareth? Philip
saith unto him, Come and
see. Jesus saw Nathanael
coming to him, and saith of
him, Behold an Israelite
indeed, in whom is no guile!
John 1:44–47

What Good Can Come from Nazareth?

Philip could hardly wait to tell somebody, and the first person he found was Nathanael. Ever since Moses they'd been saying the Messiah was just around the corner, and now he had finally turned up. Who would have guessed where? Who would have guessed who?

"Jesus of Nazareth," Philip said. "The son of Joseph." But he could hear his words fall flat.

"Can anything good come out of Nazareth?" Nathanael said.

Philip told him to come take a look for himself then, but Jesus got a look at Nathanael first as he came puffing down the road toward him, near-sighted and earnest, no doubt with his yarmulke on crooked, his dog-eared Torah under his arm.

"Behold, an Israelite indeed, in whom is no guile," Jesus said. Nathanael's jaw hung open. He said, "How do you know me?"

"Before Philip called you," Jesus said. "When you were under the fig tree, I saw you."

It was all it took apparently. "Rabbi!" Nathanael's jacket was too tight across the shoulders and you could hear a seam split somewhere as he made an impossible bow. "You are the Son of God," he said. "You are the king of Israel.

"Because I said I saw you under the fig tree, do you believe?" Jesus said. There was more to it than parlor tricks. He said, "You shall see greater things than these." But all Nathanael could see for the moment, not daring to look up, were his own two feet.

"You will see heaven opened," he heard Jesus say, "the angels of God ascending and descending upon the Son of Man." When Nathanael decided to risk a glance, the sun almost blinded him.

What Nathanael did see finally was this. It was months later, years—after the Crucifixion of Jesus. One evening he and Peter and a few of the others took the boat out fishing. They didn't get a nibble between them but stuck it out all night. It was something to do anyway. It passed the time. Just at dawn, in that queer half-light, somebody showed up on the beach and cupped his mouth with his hands. "Any luck?" The answer was No. Then give it another try, the man said. Reel in the nets and cast them off the port beam this time. There was nothing to lose they hadn't lost already, so they did it, and the catch had to be seen to be believed, had to be felt, the heft of it almost swamping them as they pulled it aboard.

Peter saw who the man was first and heaved himself overboard. The water was chest-high as he plowed through it, tripping over his feet in the shallows so he ended up scrambling ashore on all fours. Jesus was standing there waiting for him by a little charcoal fire he had going. Nathanael and the others came ashore, slowly, like men in a dream, not daring to speak for fear they'd wake up. Jesus got them to bring him some of their fish, and then they stood around at a little distance while he did the cooking. When it was done, he gave them the word. "Come and have breakfast," he said, and they sat down beside him in the sand.

Nathanael's name doesn't appear in any of the lists of the twelve apostles, but there are many who claim he was known as Bartholomew, and that name does appear there. It would be nice to think so. On the other hand, he probably considered it honor enough just to have been on hand that morning at the beach, especially considering the unfortunate remark he'd made long ago about Nazareth.

They sat there around the fire eating their fish with the sun coming up over the water behind them, and they were all so hushed and glad and peaceful that anybody passing by would never have guessed that, not long before, their host had been nailed up on a hill outside the city and left there to die without a friend to his name.

FREDERICK BUECHNER
FROM *PECULIAR TREASURES*

Nathanael saith unto him, Whence knowest thou me? Jesus answered and said unto him, Before that Philip called thee, when thou wast under the fig tree, I saw thee. Nathanael answered and saith unto him, Rabbi, thou art the Son of God; thou art the King of Israel.
John 1:48, 49

Artist Joseph Maniscalco has caught the wonder of two disciples as they struggle to pull an abundant catch into their boat. Jesus, standing on the shore, performed a small miracle by filling their nets.

Jesus Healed Them

In a world where disease and death were constant companions, where illness and blindness were mysteries, where leprosy and insanity were God's punishment for transgression, many men claimed powers of healing; and sufferers traveled far and wide in search of a miraculous cure.

When word of Jesus' healing miracles began to spread throughout Judea, some dismissed the stories as the same exaggerated and false claims they had heard before. Those who witnessed Jesus' miracles, however, believed He was the great healer the prophets had foretold. He made the blind to see, the lame to walk, the leper to lose his disease with a mere touch of His hand or a simple command from His lips.

The healer Jesus simply asked those who sought healing to believe in Him and no more. Jesus was a healer who offered more than relief from illness and pain; He offered hope.

On the west coast of the Sea of Galilee lies the city of Tiberias. In Jesus' era, the population was almost entirely Gentile; many of the residents had been brought there by force by the city's founder, Herod Antipas, who fought to populate the city with Roman citizens. Only ten miles from Capernaum, the center of Jesus' Galilean ministry, Tiberias nonetheless is never mentioned in the gospel accounts of Jesus' travels. At right is part of the old city wall.

The Master's Touch

"He touched her hand,
    and the fever left her."
He touched her hand
    as He only can,
With the wondrous skill
    of the great Physician,
With the tender touch
    of the Son of Man,
And the fever pain
    in the throbbing temples
Died out with the flush
    on brow and cheek;
And the lips that had been
    so parched and burning
Trembled with thanks
    that she could not speak;
And the eyes, where the fever
    light had faded,
Looked up—by her grateful
    tears made dim;
And she rose and ministered
    to her household—
She rose and ministered unto Him.
"He touched her hand,
    and the fever left her."
O blessed touch of the Man Divine!

AUTHOR UNKNOWN

*They entered into the house of Simon
and Andrew. . . . But Simon's wife's
mother lay sick of a fever, and anon
they tell him of her. And he came and
took her by the hand, and lifted her up;
and immediately the fever left her, and
she ministered unto them.*
Mark 1:29b–31

Our Lord

And when Jesus was entered into Capernaum, there came unto him a centurion, beseeching him, And saying, Lord, my servant lieth at home sick of the palsy, grievously tormented. And Jesus saith unto him, I will come and heal him. The centurion answered and said, Lord, I am not worthy that thou shouldest come under my roof: but speak the word only, and my servant shall be healed. When Jesus heard it, he marvelled, and said to them that followed, Verily I say unto you, I have not found so great faith, no, not in Israel. And Jesus said unto the centurion, Go thy way; and as thou hast believed, so be it done unto thee. And his servant was healed in the selfsame hour.
Matthew 8:5–8, 10, 13

Peter's mother-in-law, pictured on page thirty-four in the painting Christ Healing the Mother of Simon Peter *by J. Bridges, and all those who experienced physical contact with the Lord Jesus found the moment powerful, mysterious, and life changing.*

Jesus Christ . . . began to cure sick people by only laying his hand upon them; for God had given him power to heal the sick, and to give sight to the blind, and to do many wonderful and solemn things . . . which are called *"the miracles"* of Christ. . . . For God had given Jesus Christ the power to do such wonders; and he did them, that people might know he was not a common man, and might believe what he taught them, and also believe that God had sent him. And many people, hearing this, and hearing that he cured the sick, did begin to believe in him; and great crowds followed him in the streets and on the roads, wherever he went. . . .

There came to him a man with a dreadful disease called the leprosy. It was common in those times, and those who were ill with it were called lepers. This leper fell at the feet of Jesus Christ, and said "Lord! If thou wilt, thou cans't make me well!" Jesus, always full of compassion, stretched out his hand, and said "I will! Be thou well!" And his disease went away, immediately, and he was cured.

Being followed, wherever he went, by great crowds of people, Jesus went, with his disciples, into a house, to rest. While he was sitting inside, some men brought upon a bed, a man who was very ill of what is called the Palsy, so that he trembled all over from head to foot, and could neither stand, nor move. But the crowd being all about the door and windows, and they not being able to get near Jesus Christ, these men climbed up to the roof of the house, which was a low one; and through the tiling at the top, let down the bed, with the sick man upon it, into the room where Jesus sat. When he saw him, Jesus, full of pity, said "Arise! Take up thy bed, and go to thine own home!" And the man rose up and went away quite well; blessing him, and thanking God.

There was a Centurion too, or officer over the Soldiers, who came to him, and said "Lord! My servant lies at home in my house, very ill."—Jesus Christ made answer, "I will come and cure him." But the Centurion said "Lord! I am not worthy that Thou shoulds't come to my house. Say the word only, and I know he will be cured." Then Jesus Christ, glad that the Centurion believed in him so truly, said "Be it so!" And the servant became well, from that moment.

But of all the people who came to him, none were so full of grief and distress as one man who was Ruler or Magistrate over many people, and he wrung his hands, and cried, and said, "O Lord, my daughter—my beautiful, good, innocent little girl, is dead. O come to her, come to her, and lay thy blessed hand upon here, and I know she will revive, and come to life again, and make me and her mother happy. O Lord we love her so, we love her so! And she is dead!"

Jesus Christ went out with him, and so did his disciples and went to his house, where the friends and neighbours were crying in the room where the poor dead little girl lay, and where there was soft music playing; as there used to be, in those days, when people died. Jesus Christ, looking on her, sorrowfully, said—to comfort her poor parents—"She is not dead. She is asleep." Then he commanded the room to be cleared of the people that were in it, and going to the dead child, took her by the hand, and she rose up, quite well, as if she had only been asleep. Oh what a sight it must have been to see her parents clasp her in their arms, and kiss her, and thank God, and Jesus Christ his son, for such great Mercy!

But he was always merciful and tender. And because Jesus did such Good, and taught people how to love God and how to hope to go to Heaven after death, he was called *Our Saviour*.

CHARLES DICKENS
FROM *THE LIFE OF OUR LORD*

While he spake these things unto them, behold, there came a certain ruler, and worshipped him, saying, My daughter is even now dead: but come and lay thy hand upon her, and she shall live.

And Jesus arose, and followed him, and so did his disciples. And when Jesus came into the ruler's house, and saw the minstrels and the people making a noise, He said unto them, Give place: for the maid is not dead, but sleepeth. And they laughed him to scorn. But when the people were put forth, he went in, and took her by the hand, and the maid arose. And the fame hereof went abroad into all that land.
Matthew 9:18, 19, 23–26

Capernaum was a community of fishermen, farmers, and merchants on the northwest shore of the Sea of Galilee. No such city exists today in Israel, but scholars believe the modern city of Tell Hum occupies the ground of ancient Capernaum. The synagogue ruins pictured here date from the second or third century A.D. Because it was customary to build new synagogues on the site of the old, it is believed that the Capernaum synagogue in which Jesus taught stood on this site.

Blind Bartimaeus

As he went out of Jericho with his disciples and a great number of people, blind Bartimaeus . . . sat by the highway side begging. And when he heard that it was Jesus of Nazareth, he began to cry out, and say, Jesus, thou son of David, have mercy on me. And Jesus answered and said unto him, What wilt thou that I should do unto thee? The blind man said unto him, Lord, that I might receive my sight. And Jesus said unto him, Go thy way; thy faith hath made thee whole. And immediately he received his sight, and followed Jesus in the way.
Mark 10:46b, 47, 51, 52

Blind Bartimaeus at the gates
Of Jericho in darkness waits;
He hears the crowd—he hears a breath
Say, "It is Christ of Nazareth!"
And calls in tones of agony,
"Jesus, have mercy now on me!"

The thronging multitudes increase;
Blind Bartimaeus, hold thy peace!
But still, above the noisy crowd,
The beggar's cry is shrill and loud;
Until they say, "He calleth thee!"
"Fear not, arise, He calleth thee!"

Then saith the Christ, as silent stands
The crowd, "What wilt thou at my hands?"
And he replies, "O give me light!
Rabbi, restore the blind man's sight."
And Jesus answers, "Go in peace
Thy faith from blindness gives release!"

Ye that have eyes yet cannot see,
In darkness and in misery,
Recall those mighty Voices Three,
"Jesus, have mercy now on me!"
"Fear not, arise, and go in peace!
Thy faith from blindness gives release!"

HENRY WADSWORTH LONGFELLOW
1807–1882

Although others told him to be silent, blind Bartimaeus insisted in calling out to Jesus, who recognized the beggar's genuine faith and immediately granted him sight. Jesus' miraculous power to heal is represented at right in Carl Heinrich Bloch's painting THE MAN BORN BLIND.

And a certain woman, which had an issue of blood twelve years, And had suffered many things of many physicians, and had spent all that she had, and was nothing bettered, but rather grew worse, When she had heard of Jesus, came in the press behind, and touched his garment. For she said, If I may touch but his clothes, I shall be whole.

Mark 5:25–28

The Touch of Faith

nd his disciples said unto him, Thou seest the multitude thronging thee, and sayest thou, Who touched me?" (Mark 5:31). That is an electrifying question when you realize who asked it, and under what circumstances. You cannot escape the thrill of it—the tingle of excitement that grips you when you think of Christ stopping in response to the touch of a poor nameless woman. . . .

The incident takes place in a city street. It is a narrow twisted street packed with a crowd of gesticulating, excited people, surging past its bazaars and pavement stalls with all the noise and confusion of an eastern market place. . . . They are caught up in the infection of curiosity, and walking along in their very midst, wedged in the tightly packed procession is Someone. . . .

It is His face that will hold your gaze—and will haunt you long after the sun has gone down, and the purple night, cool and starlit, has stilled every noise in the city, while only the Syrian stars wink unsleeping.

One is aware of that face even in such a crowd. Having once seen it, one sees it everywhere, for it is a haunting face—an expression that will not fade . . . eyes whose fires never die out . . . a face that lingers in memory. Farmers were to see it as they followed the swaying plow, and fishermen were to watch it dancing on the sun-flecked water.

This One who walks like a king is named Jesus. They called Him the Nazarene or the Galilean. He called Himself the Son of man. The common people speak of Him softly, with deep affection, such as the shepherds know, who carry the little lambs in their bosoms.

The beggars whisper His name in the streets as they pass, and the children may be heard singing about Him. His name has been breathed in prayer and whispered at night under the stars. He is known to the diseased, the human flotsam and jetsam that shuffles in and out of the towns and drifts hopelessly along the dusty highways of human misery.

His name has trickled down to the streets of forgotten men, has seeped into the shadowed refuges of the unremembered women. It is Jesus of Nazareth . . . whom they are crowding to see. They want to look on His face to see the quality of His expression that seems to promise so much to the weary and the heaven-laden; that look that seems to offer healing of mind and soul and body; forgiveness of sin; another chance—a beginning again.

His look seemed to sing of tomorrow—a new tomorrow—in which there should be no more pain, no more suffering, nor persecution, nor cruelty, nor hunger, nor neglect, nor disillusionments, nor broken promises, nor death.

At the request of one Jairus, a ruler of the synagogue, He is on His way to restore to complete health a little girl. He is on a mission of restoration, and the crowd is following Him in order to see Him perform this miracle. . . .

There is in the crowd another face—the face of a woman. Strange that it should be so noticeable—yet not strange, for it is a face that portrays great depth of human emotion.

There is so much in it—pale, pinched, and wan. Great lines of suffering mar its beauty and sweetness, and even now her lips are drawn in a thin line of agony. The face is streaked with pain. Her body is racked with acute suffering.

Who is she? Well, some say her name is Martha and some say Veronica. Tradition gives her various names, but I cannot tell who she was. It does not matter. Is it not enough that she was a woman in pain? Call her Martha . . . or Mary . . . or Margaret . . . or mother . . . or sister . . . or wife. She is typical of countless cases of endless pain and suffering. For twelve years she had suffered and twelve years is a long time! Her malady seems to have been a pernicious hemorrhage or a form of bleeding cancer. She had gone to many physicians and was none better—but rather worse. She had spent all that she had, and every new day was another hopeless dawn. Every sunset was stained with the blood of her pain.

She is typical of human despair—not only physical despair but spiritual despair as well. For her the world could offer no healing—so she represents all the people who look everywhere for peace of mind and heart—for hope and comfort—and find none. She represents them all—whatever their wants, their fears, their hopes, their pains. . . .

Now this woman had heard of the Great Teacher, of His wonderful works. She had heard the lepers talk and them that had been blind from birth and now had thrown away their sticks, and looked around them with eyes that flashed or filled with tears as they spoke His name.

She had heard what He had done for others. Surely He had power to bring into the haven of health the lost explorers of the vast treasuries of pain! Surely, He had power to lift from the dust of disease the flowers whose stems had been crushed or withered in the mildews of human misery! As this thought burned itself into her mind her faith was curiously stirred as it wrestled in the birth-throes of a great resolve.

It was daring—fantastic, perhaps. Her heart thumped, but it was worth trying. It could only fail, and she was no stranger to failure. There came to the woman the assurance that if she could but touch Him—even only the hem of His garment—she would be healed of her awful malady. Cannot you imagine her nervous reasoning? "Touch Him . . . yes . . . just to touch Him—There would be no harm in that! . . .

"Besides, here is my great chance. He is coming this way; soon He will be gone. Why not touch Him as He passes? . . . It would be enough—just to touch the border of His robes. I *must* touch Him. I *must* get some of that power."

Thus reasoning, she pushes her way through the crowd and with the pertinacity of despair she struggles in that dense throng, nearer and nearer, pushing and crushing. People get in the way—not knowing her need. Now she is desperate. He must not pass so near and yet so far away. Was she to lose this opportunity? *She* must touch Him. Now just a little farther. He is drawing nearer. Now she can almost reach Him—another

And straightway the fountain of her blood was dried up; and she felt in her body that she was healed of that plague. And Jesus, immediately knowing in himself that virtue had gone out of him, turned him about in the press, and said, Who touched my clothes? And his disciples said unto him, Thou seest the multitude thronging thee, and sayest thou, Who touched me? And he looked round about to see her that had done this thing.
Mark 5:29–32

But the woman fearing and trembling, knowing what was done in her, came and fell down before him, and told him all the truth. And he said unto her, Daughter, thy faith hath made thee whole; go in peace, and be whole of thy plague.

Mark 5:33, 34

moment—at last just as He passes, she is able to reach out her hand, and with the tip of her finger touch His robe.

It was enough! She had actually touched the Great Doctor! With a trembling finger she had touched Him with the touch of a mighty faith! Like an electric shock there surged back into the shrunken veins, the panting lungs, the withered muscles, and the bloodless flesh, the rich glow of health and vitality. Once again a body had been redeemed and given life.

She had touched Him with secret and trembling haste and thrilled with the change that had come to her; she retreated back into the crowd unnoticed, she thought. No one had noticed her—no one—but Christ! Recognizing the one magnetic touch of faith amid the pressure of the crowd, He stopped and asked that *terrific* question: "Who *touched* me?"

The question seemed absurd to those who heard it. Impatiently, brusquely, almost with sarcasm, the disciples asked: "How should we know? There are hundreds of people here—pushing all about you. Look at the crowd—and yet you ask 'Who touched me?'"

But, looking around Him, Christ stood still—His kind, but searching, glance fell at last on the face of the woman who had done it.

His gaze held hers. Something passed between them, and she told Him her story while His eyes were fixed upon her; His eyes gave her confidence. They seemed to promise all that she had desired. Her fear disappeared.

Then He answered her . . . "Daughter, thy faith hath made thee whole. Go in peace . . . and be healed of thy plague."

That is the record. These are the facts. It is a matter of history. She had no money—only faith. She did not meet Him in a house of worship. She met Him on the street. She had no private audience with the Lord. She touched Him in a crowd. She touched Him in faith—in desperate believing faith and He stopped!

The touch of one anonymous woman in a crowd halted the Lord of glory. That is the glorious truth of this incident. She touched Him. So can we.

PETER MARSHALL
FROM *MR. JONES, MEET THE MASTER*

In the painting opposite, HEALING OF THE WOMAN WITH AN ISSUE OF BLOOD, the artist James J. Tissot has beautifully depicted the crush of the crowd and the desperation and weakness of the woman in the foreground who could only crawl to touch the hem of the Lord's garment.

The Woman Who Came Behind Him in the Crowd

Near him she stole, rank after rank;
She feared approach too loud;
She touched his garment's hem, and shrank,
Back in the sheltering crowd.

    A shame-faced gladness thrills her frame:
Her twelve years' fainting prayer
Is heard at last! She is the same
As other women there!

    She hears his voice. He looks about,
Ah! is it kind or good
To drag her secret sorrow out
Before that multitude?

    The eyes of the men she dares not meet—
On her they straight must fall!
Forward she sped, and at his feet
Fell down, and told him all.

    To the one refuge she had flown,
The Godhead's burning flame!
Of all earth's women she alone
Hears there the tenderest name!

    "Daughter," he said, "be of good cheer;
Thy faith hath made thee whole."
With plenteous love, not healing mere,
He comforteth her soul.

GEORGE MACDONALD
1824–1905

Christ's miraculous healings were popular subjects for artists throughout the ages. This painting, HEALING THE WOMAN WITH THE ISSUE OF BLOOD, by Venetian artist Paolo Veronese shows the renown of Christ and His disciples and the great courage that the woman must have had just to reach for His hem.

Medical Practices in Israel

Traditionally, the Jews viewed illness as punishment for disobedience of God's law; therefore, the sick turned to prayer and sacrifice for healing. The few physicians in practice were faced with deadly diseases, poor sanitation, and limited understanding of human physiology. They could offer balms, oils, healing waters, wines, and herbs, such as the wine mixed with myrrh, an ineffective painkiller, offered to Jesus on the cross. But to the seriously ill, they could offer little real hope.

And if there be in the bald head, or bald forehead, a white reddish sore; it is a leprosy sprung up in his bald head, or his bald forehead. Then the priest shall look upon it: and, behold, if the rising of the sore be white reddish in his bald head . . . He is a leprous man, he is unclean: the priest shall pronounce him utterly unclean. . . . his clothes shall be rent, and his head bare, and he shall put a covering upon his upper lip, and shall cry, Unclean, unclean.
Leviticus 13:42–45

Today, *leprosy* refers to a skin disease that is rare and controllable, if not curable. In the Bible, however, leprosy, which was diagnosed by the priests, comprised any skin disease or discoloration, and the worst cases were incurable lifelong maladies. The law of Moses concerning two colors of skin was the same as that which forbade plowing with two types of beasts or raising two different crops in the same field; and the law required that lepers be isolated as religiously unclean. Those lepers whom Jesus touched were offered not only physical relief, but spiritual healing as well.

The River Jordan flows from the foot of the 9,232-foot Mount Hermon southward into the Sea of Galilee and then on to its final destination, the Dead Sea. Between the Sea of Galilee and the Dead Sea are only sixty-five miles of territory, but the Jordan winds tortuously for two hundred miles to cover that ground. It is in most places a rough, quick-moving river, but gentle shallows do exist; it was in some of these shallows that John the Baptist conducted his ministry, baptizing, among others, Jesus of Nazareth. Pictured above is the Jordan River near Tel Beit Zaida in Israel.

Now there is at Jerusalem by the sheep market a pool, which is called in the Hebrew tongue Bethesda. . . . In these lay a great multitude of impotent folk, of blind, halt, withered, waiting for the moving of the water. For an angel went down at a certain season into the pool, and troubled the water: whosoever then first after the troubling of the water stepped in was made whole of whatever disease he had.
John 5:2–4

The healing pool of Bethesda lay in the northeastern part of Jerusalem. Tradition held that angels regularly came down and touched the pool's waters and that those who entered the water after the angels' descent would be cured of their disease. Countless men and women sought a miracle at Bethesda. The Book of John tells of one hopeful man who had been lame for thirty-eight years before traveling to Bethesda for a cure. Once at the pool, however, the man was too weak to crawl to the water and lay helpless only a short distance away. But this was the day Jesus came; and the lame man was healed, not by the waters of Bethesda, but by the Master's command.

The faithful pray at the only wall remaining of Herod's temple, the West or Wailing Wall. During Jesus' time, prayer for healing was the only hope available for the ill or lame.

In the time of Christ, stories abounded of "holy men" with miraculous powers who, through chanting, ritual, and prayers, healed the sick, lame, and insane. Jesus, however, used no chants or magic. By only a touch or a word, the lame, blind, and leprous were healed. Something else set Jesus apart from other healers: He did not want the healing to overshadow His message. Those He touched, believed; many of those who witnessed, believed; it was faith, not fame, that Jesus sought in healing.

At left are the ruins of the healing pool of Bethesda, situated in the northeastern part of Jerusalem. Archaeologists have uncovered two pools; the one shown is behind the Church of Saint Anna in the old city of Jerusalem. The man who was lame for thirty-eight years came to be healed by the waters at the pool, but instead he was healed by the word of Jesus.

The Ten Lepers

Not white and shining like an ardent flame
Not like thy mother and the saints in bliss,
But white from head to foot I bear my blame,
White as the leper is.

Unclean! unclean! But thou canst make me clean:
Yet if thou clean'st me, Lord, see that I be
Like that one grateful leper of the ten
Who ran back praising thee.

But if I must forget, take back thy word;
Be I unclean again but not ingrate.
Before I shall forget thee, keep me, Lord,
A sick man at thy gate.

KATHARINE TYNAN HINKSON
1861–1931

*There met him ten men that were
lepers, which stood afar off: And
they lifted up their voices, and said,
Jesus, Master, have mercy on us.
And when he saw them, he said
unto them, Go shew yourselves unto
the priests. And it came to pass,
that, as they went, they were
cleansed. And one of them, when he
saw that he was healed, turned
back, and with a loud voice glorified
God, And fell down on his face at
his feet, giving him thanks.*
Luke 17:12a–16a

*Although Jesus healed ten lepers on His way to
Jerusalem, only one returned to thank Him and received
Jesus' praise for his faith. In this painting by James J. Tissot entitled* HEALING OF THE TEN LEPERS, *Jesus reaches out
to the lepers, offering them relief of body and soul.*

At Even, When the Sun Was Set

And when Jesus was entered into Capernaum, there came unto him a centurion, beseeching him, And saying, Lord, my servant lieth at home sick of the palsy, grievously tormented. And Jesus saith unto him, I will come and heal him. The centurion answered and said, Lord, I am not worthy that thou shouldest come under my roof: but speak the word only, and my servant shall be healed. When Jesus heard it, he marvelled, and said to them that followed, Verily I say unto you, I have not found so great faith, no, not in Israel. And Jesus said unto the centurion, Go thy way; and as thou hast believed, so be it done unto thee.
Matthew 8:5–8, 10, 13a

The photograph opposite is of a waterfall in the Banias area of the Golan in Israel. The word Banias comes from the Roman term meaning bath.

At even, when the sun was set,
The sick, O Lord, around Thee lay;
O in what divers pains they met!
O with what joy they went away!

Once more 'tis eventide, and we,
Oppressed with various ills, draw near;
What if Thy form we cannot see,
We know and feel that Thou art here.

O Saviour Christ, our woes dispel;
For some are sick, and some are sad,
And some have never loved Thee well,
And some have lost the love they had;

And some are pressed with worldly care,
And some are tried with sinful doubt;
And some such grievous passions tear,
That only Thou canst cast them out;

And some have found the world is vain,
Yet from the world they break not free;
And some have friends who give them pain,
Yet have not sought a Friend in Thee;

And none, O Lord, have perfect rest,
For none are wholly free from sin;
And they who fain would serve Thee best
Are conscious most of wrong within.

O Saviour Christ, Thou too art Man;
Thou hast been troubled, tempted, tried;
Thy kind but searching glance can scan
The very wounds that shame would hide;

Thy touch has still its ancient power;
No word from Thee can fruitless fall;
Hear, in this solemn evening hour,
And in Thy mercy heal us all.

HENRY TWELLS
1823–1900

And, behold, there came a leper and worshipped him, saying, Lord, if thou wilt, thou canst make me clean. And Jesus put forth his hand, and touched him, saying, I will; be thou clean. And immediately his leprosy was cleansed. And Jesus saith unto him, See thou tell no man; but go thy way.
Matthew 8:2–4a

The Leper

"Room for the leper! room!" And, as he came,
The cry passed on—"Room for the leper! Room!" . . .
And aside they stood—
Matron, and child, and pitiless manhood—all
Who met him on his way—and let him pass.
And onward through the open gate he came,
A leper, with the ashes on his brow,
Sackcloth about his loins, and on his lip
A covering, stepping painfully and slow,
And with a difficult utterance, like one
Whose heart is with an iron nerve put down,
Crying, "Unclean! unclean!" . . .
—Helon was a leper!

Day was breaking,
When at the altar of the temple stood
The holy priest of God. The incense lamp
Burn'd with a struggling light, and a low chant
Swell'd through the hollow arches of the roof
Like an articulate wail, and there, alone,
Wasted to ghastly thinness, Helon knelt.
The echoes of the melancholy strain
Died in the distant aisles, and he rose up,
Struggling with weakness, and bow'd down his head
Unto the sprinkled ashes, and put off
His costly raiment for the leper's garb:
And with the sackcloth round him, and his lip
Hid in a loathsome covering, stood still,
Waiting to hear his doom:—

Depart! depart, O child
Of Israel, from the temple of thy God!
For He has smote thee with His chastening rod;
And to the desert-wild,
From all thou lov'st away, thy feet must flee,
That from thy plague His people may be free.

Depart! and come not near
The busy mart, the crowded city, more;
Nor set thy foot a human threshold o'er;
And stay thou not to hear
Voices that call thee in the way; and fly
From all who in the wilderness pass by.
Wet not thy burning lip
In streams that to a human dwelling glide;

Nor rest thee where the covert fountains hide;
Nor kneel thee down to dip
The water where the pilgrim bends to drink,
By desert well or river's grassy brink;

And pass thou not between
The weary traveller and the cooling breeze;
And lie not down to sleep beneath the trees
Where human tracks are seen;
Nor milk the goat that browseth on the plain,
Nor pluck the standing corn, or yellow grain.

And now, depart! and when
Thy heart is heavy, and thine eyes are dim,
Lift up thy prayer beseechingly to Him
Who, from the tribes of men,
Selected thee to feel His chastening rod,
Depart! O Leper, and forget not God!

And he went forth—alone! not one of all
The many whom he loved, nor she whose name
Was woven in the fibres of the heart
Breaking within him now, to come and speak
Comfort unto him. Yea—he went his way,
Sick, and heart-broken, and alone—to die!
For God had cursed the leper!

It was noon,
And Helon knelt beside a stagnant pool
In the lone wilderness, and bathed his brow,
Hot with the burning leprosy, and touched
The loathsome water to his fever'd lips,
Praying that he might be so blest—to die!

Footsteps approach'd, and with no strength to flee,
He drew the covering closer on his lip,
Crying, "Unclean! unclean!" and in the folds
Of the coarse sackcloth shrouding up his face,
He fell upon the earth till they should pass.

Nearer the Stranger came, and bending o'er
The leper's prostrate form, pronounced his name—
"Helon!" The voice was like the master-tone
Of a rich instrument—most strangely sweet;
And the dull pulses of disease awoke,
And for a moment beat beneath the hot
And leprous scales with a restoring thrill.
"Helon! arise!" and he forgot his curse,

And it came to pass, when he was in a certain city, behold a man full of leprosy: who seeing Jesus fell on his face, and besought him, saying, Lord, if thou wilt, thou canst make me clean. And he put forth his hand, and touched him, saying, I will: be thou clean. And immediately the leprosy departed from him.
Luke 5:12, 13

And rose and stood before Him.
Love and awe
Mingled in the regard of Helon's eye
As he beheld the Stranger. He was not
In costly raiment clad, nor on His brow
The symbol of a princely lineage wore;
No followers at His back, nor in His hand
Buckler, or sword, or spear—yet in His mien
Command sat throned serene, and if He smiled,
A kingly condescension graced His lips,
The lion would have crouch'd to in his lair.

His garb was simple, and His sandals worn;
His stature modell'd with a perfect grace;
His countenance, the impress of a God,
Touch'd with the open innocence of a child;
His eye was blue and calm, as is the sky
In the serenest noon; His hair unshorn
Fell to His shoulders; and his curling beard
The fulness of perfected manhood bore.

He looked on Helon earnestly awhile,
As if His heart were moved, and stooping down,
He took a little water in His hand,
And laved the sufferer's brow, and said, "Be clean,"
And lo! the scales fell from him, and his blood
Coursed with delicious coolness through his veins,
And his dry palms grew moist, and his lips
The dewy softness of an infant's stole,
His leprosy was cleansed, and he fell down
Prostrate at Jesus' feet and worshipped Him.

NATHANIEL PARKER WILLIS
1806–1867

And he charged him to tell no man: but go, and shew thyself to the priest, and offer for thy cleansing, according as Moses commanded, for a testimony unto them. But so much the more went there a fame abroad of him: and great multitudes came together to hear, and to be healed by him of their infirmities. And he withdrew himself into the wilderness, and prayed.
Luke 5:14–16

HEALING THE LEPER AT CAPERNAUM *by James J. Tissot illustrates the hope that compelled the sick to seek out Christ as well as the gentleness of Jesus as He talks with a child. Once while Jesus was at Capernaum, the crowd was so huge and so eager to meet Christ that a paralytic man was lowered down through the roof on his cot for Jesus to heal.*

Religion and Doctrine

He stood before the Sanhedrim;
The scowling rabbis gazed at him;
He recked not of their praise or blame;
There was no fear, there was no shame
For one upon whose dazzled eyes
The whole world poured its vast surprise.
The opened heaven was far too near,
His first day's light too sweet and clear,
To let him waste his new-gained ken
On the hate-clouded face of men.

But still they questioned, Who art thou?
What hast thou been? What art thou now?
Thou art not he who yesterday
Sat here and begged beside the way,
For he was blind.

And I am he;
For I was blind, but now I see.

He told the story o'er and o'er;
It was his full heart's only lore;
A prophet on the Sabbath day
Had touched his sightless eyes with clay,
And made him see, who had been blind.
Their words passed by him on the wind

Which raves and howls, but cannot shock
The hundred-fathom-rooted rock.
Their threats and fury all went wide;
They could not touch his Hebrew pride;
Their sneers at Jesus and his band,
Nameless and homeless in the land,
Their boasts of Moses and his Lord,
All could not change him by one word.

I know not what this man may be,
Sinner or saint; but as for me,
One thing I know, that I am he
Who once was blind, and now I see.

They were all doctors of renown,
The great men of a famous town,
With deep brows, wrinkled, broad and wise,
Beneath their wide phylacteries;
The wisdom of the East was theirs,
And honor crowned their silver hairs;
The man they jeered and laughed to scorn
Was unlearned, poor, and humbly born;
But he knew better far than they
What came to him that Sabbath day;
And what the Christ had done for him,
He knew, and not the Sanhedrim.

JOHN HAY
1838–1905

In John 9:1–41, Jesus heals a blind man on the Sabbath day, an act that violated the law and for which the Pharisees called Him a heretic. But Jesus was more concerned with relieving the man's suffering than in the letter of the law. At left is Martines Roerbye's painting CHRIST HEALING THE BLIND.

The Great Physician

From Thee all skill and science flow,
All pity, care, and love,
All calm and courage, faith and hope;
Oh pour them from above.

And part them, Lord, to each and all,
As each and all shall need,
To rise like incense, each to Thee,
In noble thought and deed.

And hasten, Lord, that perfect day
When pain and death shall cease,
And Thy just rule shall fill the earth
With health and light and peace.

CHARLES KINGSLEY
1819–1875

When the even was come, they
brought unto him many that were
possessed with devils: and he cast
out the spirits with his word, and
healed all that were sick.
Matthew 8:16

The painting JESUS HEALING THE LAME AND THE
BLIND *by James J. Tissot magnificently illustrates*
the crowds that must have come from all over the
country once news of the Lord's healing spread.

Jesus Taught Them

Jesus began His ministry in a society that believed the highest authority was the Law of Moses—the ten commandments and the rules of the first five books of the Old Testament. The most respected teachers were those rabbis who knew this law by heart, and who scrupulously applied it to every facet of their lives.

Jesus, however, was a teacher unlike any other. He rebuked the scholars whose obsession with the letter of the law made them slaves to ritual and blind to the spirit of the law. His principal method of teaching was the ancient, time-honored method of storytelling. These stories, or parables, conveyed deep theological truths in short, everyday speech. Even the simple and unlearned people understood what Jesus meant when He told of the prodigal son or the pearl of great price.

Jesus urged the faithful to follow God's law, not out of fear of reprisal or punishment, but out of a deep love of the Lord. He was a teacher from whom even the most studied scholars could learn, a teacher whose authority was not of this earth, but truly divine.

Pictured at right is a shallow shoreline of the Sea of Galilee, a modern name for this lake below sea level. On maps from Old Testament times it was called Lake of Chinnereth, and later, Lake Gennesaret (Luke 5:1) and then Sea of Tiberias (John 6:1).

And he opened his mouth,
and taught them, saying,
Blessed are the poor in spirit:
for their's is the
kingdom of heaven.
Blessed are they that mourn:
for they shall be comforted.
Blessed are the meek: for they
shall inherit the earth.
Blessed are they which do
hunger and thirst
after righteousness: for they
shall be filled.
Blessed are the merciful: for
they shall obtain mercy.

Matthew 5:2–7

The Divine Bliss

In the Greek there is no verb in any of the Beatitudes, which means that the Beatitudes are not statements, but exclamations. They reproduce in Greek a form of expression which is very common in Hebrew, especially in the Psalms. Hebrew has an exclamatory word *ashere*, which means: "O the bliss of . . ." So the Psalmist says: "O the bliss of the man who walks not in the counsel of the ungodly . . . but whose delight is in the law of the Lord" (Psalm 1:1). . . . This is the form of expression which each of the Beatitudes represents; each of them is an exclamation beginning: "O the bliss of . . . !" That is to say that the Beatitudes are not promises of future happiness; they are congratulations on present bliss. They are not statements and prophecies of what is one day going to happen to the Christian in some other world; they are affirmations of the bliss into which the Christian can enter even here and now. That is not to say that this bliss will not reach its perfection and its completion, when some day the Christian enters into the nearer presence of his Lord; but it is to say that even here and now the foretaste and the experience of that bliss is meant to be part of the Christian life. . . .

The promised bliss is nothing less than the blessedness of God. Through Jesus Christ the Christian comes to share in the very life of God. The bliss of the Beatitudes is another expression of what John calls Eternal Life. Eternal Life is *zoe aionios*; in Greek there is only one person in the universe to whom the word *aionios* may properly be applied, and that person is God. Eternal life is nothing less than the life of God, and it is a share in that life that Jesus Christ offers to men.

If that is so, it means that the Christian bliss is independent of outward circumstances. . . . It is independent of all the chances and the changes of life. That, indeed, is why happiness is not a good name for it. Happiness has in it the root *hap*, which means *chance*; and happiness is something which is dependent on the chances and alterations of this life; but the Christian bliss is the bliss of the life of God, and is, therefore, the joy that no man can take from us.

If this Christian bliss is the bliss of the blessedness of God, we will not be surprised to find that it completely reverses the world's standards. O the bliss of the poor! O the bliss of the sorrowful! O the bliss of the hungry and thirsty! O the bliss of the persecuted! These are startling contradictions of the world's standards; these are sayings which no man could hear for the first time without a shock of amazement. . . . But when we look at the Beatitudes carefully, we see that they are very closely interwoven into a threefold bliss.

There is the bliss which comes when a man recognizes his deepest need, and discovers where that need can be supplied. There can be three periods in any life. There can be the period when a man lives placidly and in a kind of drab mediocrity, because he knows nothing better. There can be a period of restless dissatisfaction and even of mental agony, when something makes him realize that there is an unidentified something missing in his life. And there can be the period into which there enters a new joy and a new depth into life, because a man has found that wherein his newly discovered need can be supplied. So there is bliss for the man who discovers his own poverty, for the man who becomes sorrowfully aware of his own sin, and for the man who hungers and thirsts for a righteousness which he knows is not in him.

There is the bliss of living the Christian life. There is the bliss which comes in living in mercy, in meekness, in purity of heart, and in the making of peace. These were the qualities of Jesus Christ himself, and he who follows in the steps of Jesus Christ knows the joy of the Christian life.

There is the bliss of suffering for Jesus Christ. Long ago Plato said that the good man will always choose to suffer wrong rather than to do wrong. Herein is the bliss of loyalty, and there is the deepest of all satisfactions in loyalty, even when loyalty costs all that a man has to give.

On the face of it, it might look as if the Beatitudes looked for bliss all in the wrong places; but when we think again we can see that the way of the Beatitudes is the only way to bliss.

WILLIAM BARCLAY
FROM *THE PLAIN MAN LOOKS AT THE BEATITUDES*

Blessed are the pure in heart: for they shall see God.
Blessed are the peacemakers: for they shall be called the children of God.
Blessed are they which are persecuted for righteousness' sake: for their's is the kingdom of heaven.
Blessed are ye, when men shall revile you, and persecute you, and shall say all manner of evil against you falsely, for my sake.
Rejoice, and be exceeding glad: for great is your reward in heaven: for so persecuted they the prophets which were before you.
Matthew 5:8–12

Richard Hook's painting JESUS WASHING THE DISCIPLE'S FEET illustrates the passage in John 13:4, 5: "He riseth from supper, and laid aside his garments; and took a towel, and girded himself. After that he poureth water into a bason, and began to wash the disciples' feet, and to wipe them with the towel wherewith he was girded." In Jesus' day, it was generally a servant who washed his master's feet. Thus were the apostles astonished when, after the Last Supper, Jesus knelt to wash the feet of each of them. For Jesus, however, this was a symbolic gesture meant to emphasize what He had told them many times: "the Son of man came not to be ministered unto, but to minister" (Matthew 20:28).

The typical Jewish position for teaching was sitting, not standing. According to the Book of Matthew, this is the way Jesus delivered His Sermon on the Mount. "And seeing the multitudes, he went up into a mountain: and when he was set, his disciples came unto him" (Matthew 5:1).

The Sermon on the Mount

Think not that I am come to destroy the law, or the prophets: I am not come to destroy, but to fulfil. For verily I say unto you, Till heaven and earth pass, one jot or one tittle shall in no wise pass from the law, till all be fulfilled. Whosoever therefore shall break one of these least commandments, and shall teach men so, he shall be called the least in the kingdom of heaven: but whosoever shall do and teach them, the same shall be called great in the kingdom of heaven. For I say unto you, That except your righteousness shall exceed the righteousness of the scribes and Pharisees, ye shall in no case enter into the kingdom of heaven.

Ye have heard that it hath been said, An eye for an eye, and a tooth for a tooth: But I say unto you, That ye resist not evil: but whosoever shall smite thee on thy right cheek, turn to him the other also. And if any man will sue thee at the law, and take away thy coat, let him have thy cloke also. And whosoever shall compel thee to go a mile, go with him twain. Give to him that asketh thee, and from him that would borrow of thee turn not thou away.

Ye have heard that it hath been said, Thou shalt love thy neighbour, and hate thine enemy. But I say unto you, Love your enemies, bless them that curse you, do good to them that hate you, and pray for them which despitefully use you, and persecute you; That ye may be the children of your Father which is in heaven; for he maketh his sun to rise on the evil and on the good, and sendeth rain on the just and on the unjust.

For if ye love them which love you, what reward have ye? do not even the publicans the same? And if ye salute your brethren only, what do ye more than others? do not even the publicans so? Be ye therefore perfect, even as your Father which is in heaven is perfect.

Take heed that ye do not your alms before men, to be seen of them: otherwise ye have no reward of your Father which is in heaven. Therefore when thou doest thine alms, do not sound a trumpet before thee, as the hypocrites do in the synagogues and in the streets, that they may have glory of men. Verily I say unto you, They have their reward.

But when thou doest alms, let not thy left hand know what thy right hand doeth: That thine alms may be in secret: and thy Father which seeth in secret himself shall reward thee openly.

And when thou prayest, thou shalt not be as the hypocrites are: for they love to pray standing in the synagogues and in the corners of the streets, that they may be seen of men. Verily I say unto you, They have their reward.

After this manner therefore pray ye: Our Father which art in heaven, Hallowed be thy name. Thy kingdom come. Thy will be done in earth, as it is in heaven. Give us this day our daily bread. And forgive us

Just a few miles southeast of Jesus' home village of Nazareth, Mount Tabor rises over one thousand feet to a smooth, domed peak. The mountain is named in the eighty-ninth Psalm as an example of God's glory and might, and tradition holds that it was the site of Jesus' transfiguration. At right is the lush and beautiful Galilee valley as seen from the top of Mount Tabor.

Progress

The Master stood upon the Mount, and taught.
He saw a fire in His disciples' eyes.
"The old Law," they said, "is wholly come to nought;
    Behold the new world rise!"

"Was it," the Lord then said, "with scorn ye saw
The old Law observed by Scribes and Pharisees?
I say unto you, see *ye* keep that Law
    More faithfully than these.

"Too hasty heads for ordering worlds, alas!
Think not that I to annul the Law have will'd.
No jot, no tittle, from the Law shall pass,
    Till all shall be fulfill'd."

So Christ said eighteen hundred years ago.
And what then shall be said to those today
Who cry aloud to lay the world low
    To clear the new world's way?

MATTHEW ARNOLD
1822–1888

Pictured at left is one of the many cone-shaped peaks of the Upper Golan. Ancient volcanoes, now extinct, dot the landscape; and centuries of eruptions left breathtaking views in the Upper Golan.

Now it came to pass, as they went, that he entered into a certain village: and a certain woman named Martha received him into her house. And she had a sister called Mary, which also sat at Jesus' feet, and heard his word. But Martha was cumbered about much serving, and came to him, and said, Lord, dost thou not care that my sister hath left me to serve alone? bid her therefore that she help me.

Luke 10:38–40

Sisters

ary's loveliness was twin sister to the dawn. She took the road to the village well, and as she walked, Life sang in her heart. Life—she saw it all about her—in the sun, whose strong hands pushed the mist aside and clutched the little white houses standing in huddled groups along the road, and in the very road itself stretching so comfortably before her.

Life—he felt it within her—surging up in her healthy young body, filling her with complete and unshadowed happiness. Life was so splendid a thing! Did it not hold Martha, and Lazarus, and Jesus, their Friend, who even now would be taking the road to Bethany that He might break bread with them at sundown?

As she pondered these things she lifted her face with a little gesture of expectancy, and as though she had received a command, she stood perfectly still, poised and attentive. Soon a smile of welcome illumined her face. They had come—the great unseen wings! She felt their gentle touch upon her cheeks. Always, when she thought of the Master and His Kingdom, they came. Sometimes they flew past, brushing against her lightly and quickly, leaving her filled with a great buoyancy, a great radiance of spirit, but at other times, when she was tired, when in the early evening she sat in the doorway and watched the stars, they folded and upheld her and filled her with a great peace.

She had never spoken about them to Martha. Dear, practical Martha would not understand. But the Master—*He* would understand. Very shyly she had told Him. "It is as the wings of a dove, covered with silver, and her pinions of yellow gold," He had answered her, quoting the words of the Sweet Singer of Israel. "God has gifted you with the sense of His presence."

This morning Mary felt their touch more vividly than ever, and her walk to the village wayside well became a pilgrimage to the Source of Life. . . .

Noon came out of the dawn. Yet Mary lingered. . . . Time slipped by unheeded, *and Martha waited.*

When at last Mary lifted the latch of her door, the crisp fragrance of freshly baked loaves silently reproached her tardiness. She smiled ruefully. "I'm so sorry; I forgot it was our day to use the public oven." Mary put her arms around Martha. "But life's so big, dear, and, after all, tasks are so little—like ants, hundreds and hundreds of them, one after another, in a long line from morning until night. Oh, Martha, you ought to step over them once in a while—really you ought—and just forget them, the way I do. But you're tired, dear. Go and rest now, and don't worry about preparing the evening meal, just leave it all to me."

Martha smiled dubiously and patted her younger sister in much the same manner as one pets a charming but willful child.

With the first shadows of evening, Mary stood in the doorway, watching for Jesus. It was not long before she saw Him coming along the road. . . . Mary felt a sudden sense of awe. This Man, in whom Life was so vital, so unfettered and free, this great Man with the simple, courteous manners, this Poet of a Kingdom that lay hidden within the human heart, was Lazarus' Friend and Martha's Friend, and hers! . . .

Her task lay unheeded, her resolution forgotten; and Mary sat in the doorway, talking with the Master. . . .

"The wings of a dove—have you felt them today?"

"Yes; they seemed nearer than ever before. But how did You know?"

"The story of their coming is written in your eyes."

Mary and Jesus talked on and on. Busy Martha caught the hum of their voices. Now and then, passing the doorway as she went about her tasks, her eyes grew wistful. A whole radiant world lay open to them that somehow was locked and barred to her. She tried to enter in. Could it be that she was exiled because of some subtle difference between herself and Mary? The thought pressed upon her like a dull pain.

The ache in her heart became unbearable. "Master, Master" she said, and her voice was almost a sob, "don't you care that I do all the work alone? Tell Mary to come in and help me."

Mary was startled. Martha's words fell like stones into the quiet pool of her thinking, inopportunely recalling her promise. She was about to answer Martha, to make the usual excuses, when Jesus said, His voice full of compassion: "Martha, you are troubled with many things. Mary has chosen the better part, that shall not be taken from her."

Instantly the cloud that crossed Mary's eyes gave way to an expression of relief. "That's just what I keep telling Martha. Why, if I always remembered to do the things Martha says need to be done, I would be stirring up such a noisy business, clattering pots and swishing brooms, that the beautiful wings would fly by, ever so softly, far off, in some quiet place on a little pathway, or a hillside open to the sky.

Jesus laughed. "Yes, Mary, you have chosen the better part, but there is only one way to keep it."

"How?"

"I need not tell you, for you already know."

Mary scanned His face, that of a seer and a poet; then she looked at His hands, strong and brown from having worked at countless tasks in the little carpenter shop in Nazareth; and she caught a glimpse of the working methods of Life, ever creating through dreams, and dreaming through deeds. "I believe I understand now," she said. "They are sisters, not strangers."

"Who?"

"Being and doing," she said, then rose and went in.

ELEANOR B. STOCK

And Jesus answered and said unto her, Martha, Martha, thou art careful and troubled about many things: But one thing is needful: and Mary hath chosen that good part, which shall not be taken away from her.
Luke 10:41, 42

The Pearl

I know the ways of learning; both the head
And pipes that feed the press, and make it run;
What reason hath from nature borrowèd,
Or of itself, like a good housewife, spun
In laws and policy; what the stars conspire,
What willing nature speaks, what forced by fire;
Both the old discoveries and the new-found seas,
The stock and surplus, cause and history,—
All these stand open, or I have the keys:
　　　Yet I love Thee.

I know the ways of honour, what maintains
The quick returns of courtesy and wit;
In vies of favours whether party gains;
When glory swells the heart, and mouldeth it
To all expressions both of hand and eye;
Which on the world a true-love-knot may tie,
And bear the bundle, wheresoe'er it goes;
How many drams of spirit there must be
To sell my life unto my friends or foes:
　　　Yet I love Thee.

I know the ways of Pleasure, the sweet strains,
The lullings and the relishes of it;
The propositions of hot blood and brains;
What mirth and music mean; what love and wit
Have done these twenty hundred years and more.
I know the projects of unbridled store:
My stuff is flesh, not brass; my senses live,
And grumble oft that they have more in me
Than he that curbs them, being but one to five:
　　　Yet I love thee.

I know all these, and have them in my hand:
Therefore not sealèd, but with open eyes
I fly to Thee, and fully understand
Both the main sale and the commodities;
And at what rate and price I have Thy love,
With all the circumstances that may move.
Yet through the labyrinths, not my grovelling wit
But Thy silk-twist let down from heaven to me,
Did both conduct and teach me how by it
　　　To climb to Thee.

GEORGE HERBERT
1593–1633

Again, the kingdom of heaven is like unto a merchant man, seeking goodly pearls: Who, when he had found one pearl of great price, went and sold all that he had, and bought it.
Matthew 13:45, 46

Jesus could have learned the use of parables as a boy studying in the synagogue in Nazareth. Parables are found in the writings of Plato and Aristotle, as well as in the Old Testament; and many Jewish scholars used them to provoke their students to deeper thought on the lessons of the scriptures. In the painting opposite, artist Joseph Maniscalco has depicted Jesus speaking from a boat.

Education in Jesus' Time

Jewish parents taught their children at home: girls learned about running the household and caring for the family; boys learned a trade with which they could support a family. Beginning about the first century B.C., however, boys began attending classes at synagogues at about six years of age. Here they learned to read and write, and, perhaps more importantly, they studied the ancient scriptures. This education continued until the age of ten when some boys went on to learn a trade while others continued as students of religious scholars. The Bible tells us that Jesus was a carpenter, a trade He probably learned from Joseph; but we also know that He was addressed as Rabbi, taught in the temple at age twelve, and was thoroughly grounded in the scriptures. We can assume then, that, as a boy, Jesus was a devoted student in the synagogue of Nazareth.

When Jesus began His own ministry, much of His teaching was conducted in synagogues; and He taught in the traditional method of sitting on the ground with His listeners gathered around Him and standing to read scriptures. Pictured here are the ruins of the synagogue at Capernaum.

King Solomon built the first Temple in Jerusalem for a sanctuary, a home for the ark of the covenant, and for animal sacrifices. Built on the eastern hill north of the city (where the Islamic Dome of the Rock now stands), it was completed in 950 B.C. The Temple was destroyed by fire by Babylonian King Nebuchadnezzar in 587 B.C.; thereafter, the Temple was destroyed and rebuilt, its fate reflecting that of the Jews themselves.

In 20 B.C., Herod the Great began remodeling the Temple and created a truly magnificent structure. His workmen used huge stones measuring about 40 inches deep by three to ten feet high and thirteen feet long; the Temple's walls rose 158 feet above the valley floor.

In A.D. 70, the Roman Titus captured Jerusalem and burned Herod's Temple. According to Jewish tradition, the destruction took place on the anniversary of the day that Solomon's Temple had been burned by Nebuchadnezzar more than 650 years earlier. Today, only the west wall of Herod's Temple remains standing.

Jesus told stories that illustrated divine wisdom through everyday events and used illustrations that His audience would understand. He spoke to fisherman about fishing, to farmers about farming, to shepherds about sheep. In fact, scholars use the particulars of everyday life that Jesus used for His parables to verify the facts of His life. Yet His parables are not merely simple stories. They often rise to the poetic, as in stories of the prodigal son and the good Samaritan, which not only speak of theological truths, but are literary masterpieces.

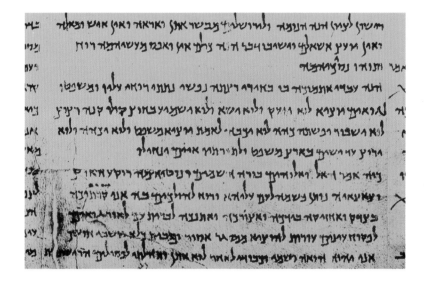

Like other children of His day, Jesus probably received early religious instruction in His local synagogue, where classes would have been conducted by a man known as the hazzan, or the keeper of the scrolls. Students in the synagogue gathered around their instructor, who sat on the open floor of the synagogue giving instruction in scripture, reading, and writing. Pictured at left is a portion of one of the two scrolls of Isaiah found in the caves of Qumram, northwest of the Dead Sea. Jesus probably studied such a scroll as a student in the synagogue.

And he taught in their synagogues . . . And he came to Nazareth, . . . and, as his custom was, he went into the synagogue on the sabbath day, and stood up for to read. And he closed the book, and he gave it again to the minister, and sat down. And the eyes of all them that were in the synagogue were fastened on him.
Luke 4:15, 16, 20

Below is a portion of the floor of the Beit Alfa Synagogue ruins in Israel.

The exact origin of the Jewish synagogue is unknown, although most scholars believe that the first synagogues were built following the destruction of Solomon's Temple in 587 B.C., either during the Babylonian exile or upon the Jews' return to Judea. The synagogue grew into a community institution, a school, a meeting place, an inn, a home for the priests, and a judicial court.

During the years of Jesus' ministry, synagogues were widespread throughout the Holy Land. Because of these local synagogues, Jesus found people well-versed in the scriptures and strong in their beliefs—fertile ground for His teachings.

And Jesus answering said, A certain man went down from Jerusalem to Jericho, and fell among thieves . . . leaving him half dead. And by chance there came down a certain priest that way: and when he saw him, he passed by on the other side. And likewise a Levite, . . . passed by on the other side. But a certain Samaritan, as he journeyed, came where he was: and when he saw him, he had compassion on him, And went to him, and bound up his wounds, pouring in oil and wine, and set him on his own beast, and brought him to an inn, and took care of him. And on the morrow when he departed, he took out two pence, and gave them to the host, and said unto him, Take care of him; and whatsoever thou spendest more, when I come again, I will repay thee. Which now of these three, thinkest thou, was neighbour unto him that fell among the thieves? And he said, He that showed mercy on him. Then said Jesus unto him, Go, and do thou likewise.

Luke 10:30–37

The parable of the good Samaritan was a reminder that Jesus' disciples should strive to uphold the spirit, not the letter of the law. The Samaritan does not think of himself, but only of the traveler in need; and it is he who lives up to Jesus' commandment: love thy neighbor. At right, artist John Walter has painted the THE GOOD SAMARITAN.

The Good Samaritan

A traveller fell among the
 thieves;
He was crushed like autumn
 leaves:
He was beaten like the sheaves
Upon the threshing-floor.

There, upon the public way,
In the shadowless heat of day,
Bleeding, stripped and bound
 he lay,
And seemed to breathe no more.

Void of hope was he, when lo!
On his way to Jericho,
Came a priest, serene and slow,
His journey just begun.

Many a silver bell and gem
Glittered on his harness' hem;
Behind him gleamed Jerusalem,
In the unclouded sun.

Broad were his phylacteries,
And his calm and holy eyes
Looked above earth's vanities,
And gazed upon the sky.

He the suffering one descried,
But, with saintly looks of pride,
Passed by on the other side,

And left him there to die.
Then approached with reverend
 pace
One of the elected race,
The chosen ministers of grace,
Who bore the ark of God.

He, a Levite, and a high
Exemplar of humanity,
Likewise passed the sufferer by,
Even as the dust he trod.

Then came a Samaritan,
A despised, rejected man,
Outlawed by the Jewish ban
As one in bonds to sin.
He beheld the poor man's need,
Bound his wounds, and with all
 speed
Set him on his own good steed,
And brought him to the inn.

When our Judge shall reappear,
Thinkest thou this man will hear,
"Wherefore didst thou interfere
With what concerned not thee?"

No! the words of Christ will run,
"Whatsoever thou hast done
To this poor and suffering one,
That hast thou done to me!"

AUTHOR UNKNOWN

The Samaritan Woman

Now Jacob's well was there. Jesus therefore, being wearied with his journey, sat thus on the well: and it was about the sixth hour. There cometh a woman of Samaria to draw water: Jesus saith unto her, Give me to drink. (For his disciples were gone away unto the city to buy meat.) Then saith the woman of Samaria unto him, How is it that thou, being a Jew, askest drink of me, which am a woman of Samaria? for the Jews have no dealings with the Samaritans. Jesus answered and said unto her, If thou knewest the gift of God, and who it is that saith to thee, Give me to drink; thou wouldest have asked of him, and he would have given thee living water.

John 4:6–10

The painting opposite is of Jesus and the woman at the well by Joseph Maniscalco. The land of Samaria lay between Galilee and Judea. Longstanding religious differences had made the Samaritans the feared enemies of Jews in Galilee and Judea. The differences centered around interpretation of the Torah and the site of the Temple. Tensions ran so high that Jews faithful to Jerusalem feared travel through Samaria. Jesus, however, ignored the hatred between His own people and the Samaritans. When He spoke to the Samaritan woman at the well, He taught by example one of His most valuable lessons: the kingdom of God is open to all who will believe.

In order to return into Galilee, Jesus could have followed the Jordan as he did on his last return, as did almost all the Jews anxious to avoid Samaria, a region despised and accursed since the Assyrian colonists had brought their idols there. The Samaritans had done worse: they had harboured a renegade priest expelled from Jerusalem, and he had built an altar on Mount Gerizim.

If Jesus followed the road through the ripening fields of Samaria, it was to meet a soul, no less defiled nor better disposed than most. Yet for this soul, and not for another, he entered the enemy territory—the first soul he was to meet, the one he was to use in order to reach many others. Near the little town of Sychar he was overcome with weariness, and he sat down by the well which Jacob had dug. His disciples went away to buy bread; he awaited their return.

The first to come happened to be a woman. There were many reasons that Jesus might not have spoken to her. First, it was not fitting for a man to speak to a woman on the road. And then he was a Jew and she was a Samaritan. And then he who knew hearts—and bodies too—was not unaware of the identity of this graceful being. . . .

She might fully be what she was: a concubine, a woman who had dragged in the mire, passed from one to another, who had lain in the arms of six men, and he whose thing she now was, and who tasted pleasure with her, was not her husband. Jesus took what he found, gathered up no matter what, that his Kingdom might come. He looked at her and decided that on that very day this creature would seize Sychar in his name and would found in Samaria the kingdom of God. . . . Jesus looked at her closely; he had not that haughty air, that contraction of the virtuous before a woman who made a business of love. Neither did he look at her with indulgence, nor with connivance. She was a soul, the first to come, of which he was going to make use. A ray of sun lay across a potsherd in the dirt heap, the flame leaped up, and all the forest caught fire.

The sixth hour. It was hot. The woman heard some one call her. Was the Jew speaking to her? But yes; he said: "Give me to drink." At once coy and mocking, she replied to the perspiring stranger:

"How dost thou, being a Jew, ask to drink of me, who am a Samaritan?"

"If thou didst know the gift of God, and who he is who saith to thee, 'Give me to drink,' thou wouldst have asked of him, and he would have given thee living water."

Christ brooked no delay; his words were incomprehensible to the Samaritan woman, but like a thief he had already entered into that dark soul. She must have felt besieged on every side, and the stranger whose dripping face and dusty feet she saw before her entered into her soul, invaded her, and she was powerless before this living surge. Dumfounded, she ceased to mock, and . . . began to ask childish questions:

The woman saith unto him, Sir, thou hast nothing to draw with, and the well is deep: from whence then hast thou that living water? Art thou greater than our father Jacob, which gave us the well, and drank thereof himself, and his children, and his cattle? Jesus answered and said unto her, Whosoever drinketh of this water shall thirst again: But whosoever drinketh of the water that I shall give him shall never thirst; but the water that I shall give him shall be in him a well of water springing up into everlasting life.

John 4:11–14

"Sir, thou hast no pail and the well is deep; whence then hast thou living water? Art thou greater than our father Jacob, who gave us this well, and drank thereof himself, and his sons and his cattle?"

Jesus had no time to lose; he was going to thrust her, with an impatient gesture, into the full glare of the truth. He said:

"Everyone that drinketh of this water shall thirst again; but whosoever drinketh of the water that I shall give him shall never thirst, but the water that I shall give him shall become in him a fountain of water springing up into everlasting life."

Every word of the Lord should be taken to the letter. That is why many have believed themselves drunk with this water and have been deceived; this was not the water of which Jesus spoke, since having drunk of it they thirsted still. Nevertheless, the woman replied:

"Sir, give me this water, that I may not thirst, nor come hither to draw."

"Go, call thy husband and come hither."

Always the same methods to persuade the simple: the same method he used with Nathanael when he said: "I saw thee under the fig tree." It revealed to them at once his knowledge of their lives, or rather his power to take up his abode within them, to enter into their most secret being; and that is why when the Samaritan woman said, "I have no husband," he replied:

"Thou hast said rightly, 'I have no husband': for thou hast had five husbands, and now he whom thou hast is not thy husband. This hast thou said truly."

The woman did not belong to the royal race of Nathanael and Simon, of those who immediately fell on their knees and struck their breasts. She was at first only a guilty woman caught in her sin, and, in order to divert the attention of this Rabbi who knew too much, she tried to put the discussion on a theological basis. After having stammered, "Sir, I perceive that thou art a prophet . . ." she added hastily:

"Our fathers worshipped on this mountain; yet ye say that the right place for worship is Jerusalem."

Jesus did not allow himself to be turned away; he laid aside the objection with several words. But he was pressed for time; the disciples were returning with provisions. He heard them talking and laughing. They must not come there until he had finished. The truth must be given this poor woman at once:

"The hour cometh and now is, when true worshippers shall worship the Father in spirit and truth. For indeed the Father seeketh such worshippers. God is a spirit; and those who worship him must worship in spirit and truth."

And the Samaritan woman: "I know that Messiah is coming; when he cometh, he shall declare unto us all things."

Already the disciples' steps could be heard on the road. To hear the secret he had never yet told anyone, Jesus chose this woman who had had five husbands and who then had a lover.

"I that speak with thee am he."

And at that very moment, the light of grace was given to the miserable woman; so strong was it that no doubt could ever assail her. Yes, this poor burdened Jew who had walked far in the sun and the dust and who so suffered from thirst that he must beg a little water from a woman of Samaria, was the Messiah, the Saviour of the world.

She stood there petrified, until she heard the voices of those who accompanied this man, coming nearer. Then she started to run, like one whose garments were on fire. She entered Sychar to arouse the people. She cried:

"Come and see a man who hath told me all that I have done."

One would have said that Christ, still seated on the edge of the well, while his disciples gave him a morsel of bread, had trouble in returning to their narrow world. "Rabbi, eat!" they insisted. But incarnate love, unmasked by this woman, had not yet had time to become a man again, a man who hungered and thirsted.

"I have food to eat that ye know not."

This answer still came from another world. The poor people imagined that someone had brought him mysterious food to eat. He looked at their staring eyes, their gaping mouths, and beyond in the blinding light the harvest fields of Samaria, with their ripening ears of corn. Above the corn, heads were moving: a troop of people led on by the woman (her lover was perhaps among them!).

Finally, Jesus touched earth again. He spoke of the things of the soil which they knew, quoted a proverb, reassured them, led them to understand that they would reap what he had sown. He had already made them fishers of men, now they would be harvesters of human sheaves.

He tarried for two days in the midst of the outcast Samaritans, thus giving his followers an example which was to be transmitted in vain to the rest of the world. For if there is a part of the Christian message which men have refused and rejected with invincible obstinacy, it is faith in the equal value of all souls, of all races, before the Father who is in heaven.

FRANÇOIS MAURIAC
FROM *LIFE OF JESUS*

Jesus saith unto her, Woman, believe me, the hour cometh, when ye shall neither in this mountain, nor yet at Jerusalem, worship the Father. Ye worship ye know not what: we know what we worship: for salvation is of the Jews. But the hour cometh, and now is, when the true worshippers shall worship the Father in spirit and in truth: for the Father seeketh such to worship him. God is a Spirit: and they that worship him must worship him in spirit and in truth. The woman saith unto him, I know that Messias cometh, which is called Christ: when he is come, he will tell us all things. Jesus saith unto her, I that speak unto thee am he.
John 4:21-26

Jesus Amazed Them

During many periods throughout history, and especially in Jesus' time, people viewed natural events as signs of God's power over His creation. When floods, plagues, storms, and droughts ravaged the land, they were seen as expressions of God's wrath and displeasure at the transgressions of His people. Equally, good crops, favorable weather, and propitious rainstorms were taken as expressions of God's favor.

The people looked to nature for signs at all times; the Magi from the East found a sign in the heavens that led them to the newborn Jesus. Nature was, in effect, God's language of communication to His people. Those who witnessed Jesus walking on water, quieting the raging sea, and causing the fig tree to wither were amazed and believed He was the Son of God, for only God Incarnate could display such mastery over God's natural creation.

The photograph at right offers a serene view of the Sea of Galilee. The lake's approximately thirty-two miles of shoreline are skirted by steep hills; and cool winds often rush down the slopes, creating violent waves on the lake's warm surface. A storm such as this was easily calmed at Jesus' command.

Water into Wine

Elizabeth rose and dressed carefully. . . . Some time during the morning would come the ceremonious entrance of the messengers from Philip [her betrothed] bearing her bridal dress and ornaments and the ointment and perfumes.

There was no breakfast to make, for she must fast until evening. But there were the prayers of Atonement with which her mind must be occupied most of the day. She knelt facing Jerusalem and recited softly the solemn, stately words of the confession. Later the messengers arrived. The bridal gown with all its expensive ornaments was spread upon the bed. She smiled tenderly at Philip's extravagance. He had sent perfumes enough for a lifetime.

In the early evening, while the neighbors swarmed about the rooms, trying to be helpful, Elizabeth stood before her mirror and let down her long black hair until it fell about her shoulders as a maiden bride's must hang. They helped her into her bridal dress, exclaiming at its beauty. With her own hands Elizabeth adjusted the "attire" about her waist and the crown of fresh myrtle leaves that she had preferred to the golden imitation. Then over all was thrown the long white veil of betrothal that would not be raised until Philip's own hands lifted it in the hush of the bridal chamber. Elizabeth was ready.

The early dusk had grown swiftly to darkness. The young girls who had been running in and out were gone hastily to their own homes to don their last bit of finery for the procession.

A shout came from the doorway. "Here they come! Look! Thou canst see the torches! And the flutes! Dost thou hear them? Oh, it will be a great procession. Call Elizabeth. Tell her they have started!"

The sounds came clearly through the night. Philip and his groomsmen were on their way to her. The neighbors were all thronging the streets. The maidens were waiting, ready to circle about her when she emerged from the house. All at

And the third day there was a marriage in Cana of Galilee; and the mother of Jesus was there: And both Jesus was called, and his disciples, to the marriage. And when they wanted wine, the mother of Jesus saith unto him, They have no wine. Jesus saith unto her, Woman, what have I to do with thee? mine hour is not yet come. His mother saith unto the servants, Whatsoever he saith unto you, do it.

John 2:1–5

Jewish weddings in Jesus' day were often held at harvesttime with music, dancing, and feasting. The betrothal, which generally happened a year before the wedding feast, was the official ceremony of marriage. There the parents, who had arranged the marriage, made the formal agreements that bound their children. The painting on the previous page is an elaborate depiction of Christ's first miracle, THE MARRIAGE FEAST AT CANA, *from an unknown artist of the Venetian school of Italian painters.*

once the shouting increased deafeningly. The torches again became a confused glare. They had reached her house. Elizabeth felt herself conducted through lines of laughing, bowing men and women on to the doorway, where Philip met her and drew her inside.

He led her proudly to the room reserved for the women and seated her on the soft-rug-covered dais prepared for her. The other women and maidens who were invited to the house crowded in and found seats on the floor and cushioned ledges. Through the door which led into the room where the feast was spread for the men, and where the singing and dancing would take place, Elizabeth could see the women who were to serve, carrying food to the table and chatting importantly to each other as they worked. She watched the form of Mary of Nazareth as she came and went. So gentle in her movements, so quiet of speech, so tender and smiling as she looked upon the group that clustered round the bridegroom.

Then Terenth came in with refreshments for the women. "There are many strangers," she commented, excitedly. "Four men are sitting with Nathanael, and he keeps calling one of them Rabbi. He is Mary's son from Nazareth, but I didn't know He was a rabbi. Philip's father is so excited. We can't bring things in fast enough to please him. He is mightily lavish with the wine. Philip will have to go clear to the new vineyards for more for tomorrow night. Thou shouldst see how the guests eat!"

She ran out, laughing, but it seemed only a moment until she was back with blanched face. *"The wine is gone!"* she gasped. "There isn't another drop and the feast but barely begun! We thought there were two more vats of it and they are empty! What can we do?"

At the first words Elizabeth had started in surprise. Now she sat tense with hands gripped together. No more wine! The feast begun in riotous plenty was to end in poverty and disgrace. . . . "Tell Mary of Nazareth!" she whispered. "She is always calm and wise. She will know how to tell the governor and the rest when it has to be known."

When Terenth had rushed away and the chatter of awed comment and criticism and speculation was in full flow about her, Elizabeth sat speechless and stunned behind her veil.

This was no small calamity that was about to fall upon them. It was a lifelong disgrace for Philip and his father. Never again could they hold up their heads in the village. No matter whose mistake it had been, the burden of reproach would rest upon them. And no one would ever let them forget it. This flagrant breach of hospitality, this unprecedented failure to make good the promise of their lavish invitations. No apology could be offered or accepted. There would be only the ugly fact to speak for itself. There would be a little while of forced merriment and then the guests would go. And Philip and his father would be left amid the ruins of the feast and the bitterness of their disgrace.

Suddenly she noticed that the women and maidens had stopped talking. A silence had fallen upon the feast-room, too. Elizabeth caught her breath. Some one must be telling Philip and his father now. For a long second the strange hush lasted. And then everything was as it had been before. The talking, the laughter, the women running to and fro with their platters and pitchers. And high above the other voices rose the strong tones of the governor of the feast.

"How is this, Philip?" he was demanding. "Every man when he maketh a feast doth first serve the good wine, and then when men have well drunk, he serveth that which is worse. But thou hast kept the *good* wine until now!"

The governor sounded well pleased. Then Philip replied, his voice still vibrant with pride and joy: "But, governor, is the best not worth waiting for always?"

Then overwhelmingly rose the shouts: "To the bridegroom! Fill your cups and drink again to the bridegroom! Joy to Philip and his bride!"

One of the maidens leaned cautiously toward the door of the feast-room. "They *have* wine! They are drinking it now. Terenth is silly and excitable. Alarming us for naught. Wait till she comes again! We shall teach her a lesson."

But Terenth was already there. "There has been a *miracle*. There is a man of God in this house!" Then, before the excited gasps of wonder had become coherent, Terenth went on: *"There was no wine.* Any of the women or the servants will tell you that. I did as Elizabeth bade me. I asked Mary of Nazareth to break the news to Philip and his father. I was just behind her as she entered the room. Instead of going to the end of the table she stopped beside her Son. I heard her whisper to Him: 'They have no wine'—only that. But she looked at Him beseechingly. Her Son looked grave for a moment and then He smiled a little and said in the gentlest voice: 'Woman, what have I to do with thee? Mine hour is not yet come.' But she smiled back at Him and touched His shoulder—they must love each other deeply, those two—and signed to a servant. 'Do whatever he telleth thee' she said.

"Then this Jesus told the servant to fill the six big water-jars in the hallway, full of water. When it was done he said quietly: 'Draw out now and bear to the governor of the feast!'

"And as we drew, *the water was changed to wine!* They are drinking it now."

In the midst of it all, Elizabeth sat withdrawn, apart, trying to sense the awesome thing she had just heard. Under this roof, Philip's roof, which was now her home, *water had been changed into wine!* That quiet guest in the other room had wrought a *miracle!* God was dwelling in this place.

AGNES SLIGH TURNBULL
FROM *FAR ABOVE RUBIES*

Jesus saith unto them, Fill the waterpots with water. And they filled them up to the brim. And he saith unto them, Draw out now, and bear unto the governor of the feast. And they bare it. When the ruler of the feast had tasted the water that was made wine, and knew not whence it was: . . . the governor of the feast called the bridegroom, And saith unto him, Every man at the beginning doth set forth good wine; and when men have well drunk, then that which is worse: but thou hast kept the good wine until now. This beginning of miracles did Jesus in Cana of Galilee, and manifested forth his glory; and his disciples believed on him.

John 2:7–11

Jesus then lifted up his eyes, and saw a great company come unto him, One of his disciples, Andrew, . . . saith unto him, There is a lad here, which hath five barley loaves, and two small fishes: but what are they among so many? . . . And Jesus took the loaves; and when he had given thanks, he distributed to the disciples, and the disciples to them . . . and likewise of the fishes as much as they would. When they were filled, he said unto his disciples, Gather up the fragments that remain, that nothing be lost. Therefore they gathered them together, and filled twelve baskets with the fragments of the five barley loaves, which remained over and above unto them that had eaten. Then those men, when they had seen the miracle that Jesus did, said, This is of a truth that prophet that should come into the world.

John 6:5a, 8, 9, 11–14

The miracle of the loaves and fishes is the only miracle recounted in all four gospels. The situation arose because of the great throngs of people who had begun to follow Jesus everywhere He went—some seeking healing, others just curious about this Man from Nazareth. Opposite, the Limbourg Brothers, Flemish artists from the fifteenth century, depict BOOK OF HOURS: FEEDING THE MULTITUDES.

The Boy with the Five Loaves

What time the Saviour spread His feast
For thousands on the mountain's side,
One of the last and least
The abundant store supplied.

Haply, the wonders to behold,
A boy 'mid other boys he came,
A lamb of Jesus' fold,
Though now unknown by name.

Well may I guess how glow'd his cheek,
How he look'd down, half pride, half fear
Far off he saw one speak
Of him in Jesus' ear.

"There is a lad—five loaves hath he,
And fishes twain:—but where are they
Where hungry thousands be?"
Nay, Christ will find a way.

In order, on the fresh green hill,
The mighty Shepherd ranks his Sheep
By tens and fifties, still
As clouds when breezes sleep.

Oh, who can tell the trembling joy,
Who paint the grave endearing look,
When from that favoured boy
The wondrous pledge He took?

Thou prayest without the veil as yet:
But kneel in faith: an arm benign
Such prayer will duly set
Within the holiest shrine.

And Prayer has might to spread and grow.
Thy childish darts, right-aim'd on high,
May catch Heaven's fire and glow
Far in the eternal sky:

Even as He made that stripling's store
Type of the Feast by Him decreed,
Where Angels might adore,
And souls for ever feed.

JOHN KEBLE
1792–1866

Natural Signs and Wonders

There are instances in the Old Testament when the truly miraculous took place in the natural world. The sun stood still to give Joshua and his army more time in battle. The Red Sea parted so that Moses could lead the Israelites out of captivity in Egypt, and then receded to drown Pharaoh's army. Joshua and Moses called upon God to work these natural miracles. Jesus, however, worked miracles by His own authority over the forces of nature.

Pictured here is a star of David on part of the ruins of old Jericho. Jericho is one of the oldest settlements in the world, with archeological remains dating back ten thousand years. The city's rich history includes the story of the city's conquest in Joshua chapter 6. After faithfully following God's instructions, Joshua and his army watched the walls of Jericho tumble, tangible evidence of God's miraculous power.

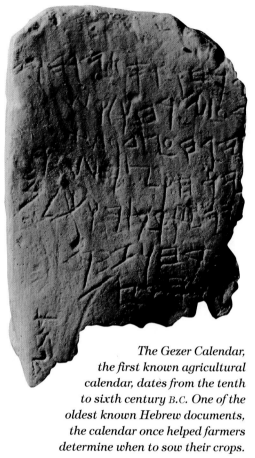

The Gezer Calendar, the first known agricultural calendar, dates from the tenth to sixth century B.C. One of the oldest known Hebrew documents, the calendar once helped farmers determine when to sow their crops.

Then spake Joshua to the LORD . . . and he said in the sight of Israel, Sun, stand thou still upon Gibeon; and thou, Moon, in the valley of Ajalon. And the sun stood still, and the moon stayed, until the people had avenged themselves upon their enemies. And there was no day like that before it or after it, that the LORD hearkened unto the voice of a man.
Joshua 10:12, 13a, 14a

The people Jesus taught were, for the most part, farmers, fishermen, or shepherds. They grew grain, grapes, olives, and figs and tended sheep, goats, and occasionally cattle. Much of Judea is desert; but even in the fertile Jordan River valley, people were dependent upon nature for their survival. They believed a merciful God sent rain; a fierce storm came from God's wrath. In an ever-changing natural world, they read the judgment of God upon their worthiness. For these people, Jesus, who demonstrated His mastery over the powerful forces of nature, was truly the Son of God.

Jesus displayed His lordship over the natural world by calming a storm, walking on water, turning water into wine, and feeding thousands from a handful of loaves and fishes. But nowhere in the Bible does nature bow so low as on the day of the Crucifixion. The sky turned dark for three hours until Jesus died, a great earthquake shook the city, stones were broken, the huge temple veil was torn in half, and graves were opened so the resurrected could walk among their kinsmen. Here was physical evidence that the world and all nature remained under His command. Here was real evidence of not only the power and the might of God, but of the love and compassion for His Son and all mankind.

Fishing methods and equipment have changed little in two thousand years; and it is easy to imagine Peter, James, Andrew, and John perhaps fishing the same waters in a boat similar to the one pictured, casting their nets into the Sea of Galilee.

And the LORD said unto Moses, Stretch out thine hand over the sea, that the waters may come again upon the Egyptians, upon their chariots, and upon their horsemen. And Moses stretched forth his hand over the sea.
Exodus 14:26–27a

And he left them, and went out of the city into Bethany; and he lodged there. Now in the morning as he returned into the city, he hungered. And when he saw a fig tree in the way, he came to it, and found nothing thereon, but leaves only, and said unto it, Let no fruit grow on thee henceforward for ever. And presently the fig tree withered away. And when the disciples saw it, they marvelled, saying, How soon is the fig tree withered away! Jesus answered and said unto them, Verily I say unto you, If ye have faith, and doubt not, ye shall not only do this which is done to the fig tree, but also if ye shall say unto this mountain, Be thou removed, and be thou cast into the sea; it shall be done. And all things, whatsoever ye shall ask in prayer, believing, ye shall receive.

Matthew 21:17–22

Israel varies from fertile farmland to thick forests to river valleys to semi-arid desert. In Galilee, where Jesus began His ministry, the soil was rich and yielded grains, vegetables, nuts, and fruits. In Judea, the land was dry and rocky; agriculture took the form of nomadic herding of sheep and goats. But everywhere, the people respected the power of nature, for their livelihoods were at its mercy. When Jesus displayed His lordship over the natural world, calming the storm and making the fig tree wither, the farmers and herdsmen of the Holy Land took notice. On the opposite page, a lone palm and a herd of goats share a stretch of the Judean wilderness.

Miracle

He was on His way from Bethany to Jerusalem,
Languishing under the sadness of premonitions.

The slope's prickly scrubwood had been scorched by the sun;
No smoke rose from a near-by hut.
The air was hot; the reeds did not stir
And the calm of the Dead Sea was unbroken.

And, knowing a bitterness that rivalled the bitterness of the sea,
Accompanied only by a small band of clouds,
He went on along the dusty road
Intent on reaching a certain religious school.
He was on His way to attend a gathering of disciples.
And so deeply was He plunged in His thoughts
That the countryside sent forth an odor of wormwood.
A stillness fell over all things. He stood alone
In the midst of it all. And all the region lay prostrate
As if in a swoon. All things became confused:
The sultriness and the desert,
And lizards, and wellsprings and streams.

A fig tree rose up a short distance ahead—
Utterly fruitless, putting forth only branches and leaves.
And He said unto it: "Of what use art thou?
What joy have I from thee, standing there petrified?
I am enhungered and athirst, yet thou art all barren
And coming upon thee is of less joy than stumbling on granite.
Oh, how thou dost offend, how void of any gift!
Remain, then, even as thou art until the end of time."

A shudder at the condemnation ran through the tree
Even as a spark of lightning runs down a rod.
The fig tree was instantly consumed to ashes.

If at that point but a moment of free choice had been granted
To the leaves, the branches, to the trunk and roots
The laws of nature might have contrived to intervene.

But a miracle is a miracle—and miracle is God.
When we are in confusion, then in the midst of our straggling
It overtakes us and, on the instant, confounds us.

BORIS PASTERNAK
1890–1960

Christ Stilling the Tempest

Fear was within the tossing bark,
    When stormy winds grew loud;
And waves came rolling high and dark,
    And the tall mast was bowed:

And men stood breathless in their dread,
    And baffled in their skill—
But One was there, who rose and said
    To the wild sea, "Be still!"

And the wind ceased—it ceased!—that word
    Passed through the gloomy sky;
The troubled billows knew their Lord,
    And sank beneath his eye.

And slumber settled on the deep,
    And silence on the blast,
As when the righteous falls asleep,
    When death's fierce throes are past.

Thou that didst rule the angry hour,
    And tame the tempest's mood,
Oh! send thy spirit forth in power,
    O'er our dark souls to brood!

Thou that didst bow the billows' pride
    Thy mandates to fulfill,
Speak, speak, to passion's raging tide,
    Speak and say—"Peace, be still!"

FELICIA DOROTHEA HEMANS
1793–1835

And the same day, when the even was come, he saith unto them, Let us pass over unto the other side. And when they had sent away the multitude, they took him even as he was in the ship. And there were also with him other little ships. And there arose a great storm of wind, and the waves beat into the ship, so that it was now full. And he was in the hinder part of the ship, asleep on a pillow: and they awake him, and say unto him, Master, carest thou not that we perish? And he arose, and rebuked the wind, and said unto the sea, Peace, be still. And the wind ceased, and there was a great calm. And he said unto them, Why are ye so fearful? how is it that ye have no faith? And they feared exceedingly, and said one to another, What manner of man is this, that even the wind and the sea obey him?

Mark 4:35–41

The magnificent painting opposite by Rembrandt Van Rijn, THE STORM ON THE SEA OF GALILEE, shows us the power of the storm and the overwhelming danger the apostles faced on the Sea of Galilee, making the calm that followed Jesus' words, "Peace, be still," even more remarkable.

Walking on the Sea

When the storm on the mountains
    of Galilee fell,
And lifted its water on high;
And the faithless disciples were bound
    in the spell
Of mysterious alarm—their terrors to quell,
Jesus whispered, "Fear not, it is I."

The storm could not bury that word in the wave,
For 'twas taught through the tempest to fly;
It shall reach his disciples in every clime,
And his voice shall be near
    in each troublous time,
Saying, "Be not afraid, it is I."

When the spirit is broken
    with sickness or sorrow,
And comfort is ready to die;
The darkness shall pass,
    and in gladness tomorrow,
The wounded complete consolation
    shall borrow
From his life-giving word, "It is I."

When the waters are passed,
    and the glories unknown
Burst forth on the wondering eye,
The compassionate "Lamb in the midst
    of the throne"
Shall welcome, encourage, and comfort his own,
And say, "Be not afraid, it is I."

NATHANIEL HAWTHORNE
1804–1864

Jesus Saved Them

Throughout the Gospels of the New Testament, Jesus Christ met people who asked, in one form or another, the same question asked by Nicodemus, "What must I do to have eternal life?" And to each, the answer Jesus gave was the same: "Ye must be born again."

Like Nicodemus, the thief on the cross confessed belief in the Son of God and was given the assurance that on that day he would be with Christ in paradise. Likewise Zacchaeus, a corrupt tax collector, invited Jesus into his home and was reborn into a life of righteousness. All found new life through their faith in Jesus.

Some who met Jesus, however, chose to reject His love. The rich young ruler would not sell all he had and follow Jesus. Pilate and Caiaphas were so close to the truth yet were unable or unwilling to grasp Christ's message.

Christ's message to them was His message to us all: He had come to earth to offer redemption to mankind. All He asked was complete faith, through which anyone, sinner or saint, could be transformed and born again to eternal life.

Shepherds and sheep are mentioned more than three hundred times in the Bible, and the work of the shepherd was familiar to most people living in Israel at the time of Jesus. Thus, Jesus was drawing upon fertile imagery when He called Himself the "Good Shepherd" who would lay down His life for His flock. At right, a shepherd tends his flock in modern-day Israel.

The Rich Young Man

And a certain ruler asked him, saying, Good Master, what shall I do to inherit eternal life? And Jesus said unto him, Why callest thou me good? none is good, save one, that is, God. Thou knowest the commandments, Do not commit adultery, Do not kill, Do not steal, Do not bear false witness, Honour thy father and thy mother. And he said, All these have I kept from my youth up. Now when Jesus heard these things, he said unto him, Yet lackest thou one thing: sell all that thou hast, and distribute unto the poor, and thou shalt have treasure in heaven: and come, follow me.

Luke 18:18–22

hildren were not the only ones who caused his heart to beat. With the audacity of youth, a boy interrupted him, saying: "Master, what am I to do to inherit life everlasting?" Jesus, without at first taking thought of him to whom he spoke, replied: "Thou knowest the commandments." He named them.

And the young man: "Master, all these have I kept from my youth."

This was said no doubt in a tone of simplicity, of humility, which touched Christ. Then only he lifted his eyes to him who spoke. "Jesus looked on him and loved him." After having looked at him . . . a certain expression touched the Son of Man, the grace of a young person, the light in his eyes which came from the soul. He loved him therefore, and like a God to whom all are subject, without preparation, almost brutally, he said:

"One thing is lacking to thee: go, sell all thou hast and give to the poor—and thou shalt have treasure in heaven—and come, follow me."

If Jesus had not loved him . . . no doubt he would have granted this young man the strength to leave all, as others had done. He would have submitted him to all-powerful grace. But love does not wish to obtain anything from him who is loved, unless it be freely given. He loved this stranger too much to capture him by force. From him the Son of Man hoped for a spontaneous movement of the heart. "But his face fell at the saying, and he departed grieved, for he had great possessions."

He was swallowed up in a crowd and with his eyes Jesus followed him far beyond space, into the depths of time, from misery to misery. For those whom Christ calls and who turn away, fall, lift themselves up, drag themselves about with eyes full of heavenly light, but with their garments stained, their hands torn and bleeding.

The sorrow which Jesus felt betrayed itself in the vehemence of [words] against the rich, which fell almost immediately from his lips. "With what difficulty shall they that have riches enter the kingdom of God . . . easier for a camel to pass through the eye of a needle."

Who, then, can be saved? Torturing thought for the saints themselves. His friends' sadness touched Jesus. Because he was the Son of God, the Author of life, he was going to destroy with one word all that he had said (perhaps also he saw in spirit that final moment when the young being who was turning away would come back to him of his own accord). "With men it is impossible . . . all things are possible with God." Even to save as many rich men as he pleased to save, even to bring back those creatures who have fallen the lowest, to take them by force, to gather to himself a soul, still begrimed, from the lips of a dying man. All things are possible with God; this is as literally true as all the other words of the Lord. All! He had already said: "I will draw all men to myself!" O, divine and hidden stratagem of that mercy which knows no control nor limit! All things are possible with God.

Jesus' severity frightened the Apostles, but his indulgence made them jealous. What now? Then all the world would be saved? And we?

Peter murmured: "Behold, we have left all things and have followed thee."

Jesus covered them with a glance that reached beyond them and saw, throughout the ages, the innumerable multitude of consecrated and crucified souls.

"Amen I say to you, no one hath left home, or brothers, or sisters, or mother, or father, or children, or lands, for my sake and for the sake of the gospel, but shall receive a hundred-fold now in this time, houses, and brother, and sisters, and mothers, and children, and lands—together with persecutions—and in the world to come life everlasting."

FRANÇOIS MAURIAC
LIFE OF JESUS

The painting by artist Heinrich Hoffmann entitled RICH MAN WHO WENT AWAY SORROWFUL *perfectly captures the haughty arrogance of the "certain ruler" of Luke 18 who asked Jesus what he must do to have eternal life. Unable to sacrifice his great wealth, the rich man chose worldly riches over following the Lord.*

A Parable for Public Officials

And, behold, there was a man named Zacchaeus, which was the chief among the publicans, and he was rich. And he sought to see Jesus who he was; and could not for the press, because he was little of stature. And he ran before, and climbed up into a sycamore tree to see him: for he was to pass that way. And when Jesus came to the place, he looked up, and saw him, and said unto him, Zacchaeus, make haste, and come down; for to day I must abide at thy house. And he made haste, and came down, and received him joyfully.

Luke 19:2–6

 t a time when many public officials are under charges of betraying their country, and business leaders of creating monopolies with restraint of trade, and labor leaders of confiscating union dues for their personal profit, it may be worth recalling the history of a very famous public official who suddenly turned and became a worthy citizen. His name was Zacchaeus, and his particular official title was publican. A publican worked for the Income Tax Bureau of the Roman government in Judea. He was a despised citizen, not just because he was an income tax collector, but because he was also a traitor. Just as some Americans betray their country to help Russia enslave the world, so Zacchaeus deserted his own people to serve the conquerors of his native land.

Zacchaeus did not trouble much about getting mink coats for his wife, but he was tremendously concerned with "kickbacks." He would collect in our money, say, $500,000 from a given area, give $100,000 of that to the foreign conquerors, and pocket the rest himself. Reputation is what men *say* about us, character is what a man *is*. No one spoke kindly about this "crook" but at heart he seemed to have very good instincts. The story of his transformation is familiar. One day when the Divine Saviour came to His native town of Jericho, Zacchaeus tried to see Him. Being a "shorty" he could not look over the heads of the crowd, so he climbed into a sycamore tree. One cannot imagine the Director of the Tax Bureau of any great city climbing a tree to see a parade, or to catch a glimpse of a visitor, but apparently Zacchaeus was more humble. When a man begins looking for God, he will soon discover that God is looking for him.

The Good Lord looked up and called him by name, and then said: "Make haste and come down; I am to lodge today at thy house." The artificial elevation where our pride has thrust us, or the false compensations we make by climbing trees of egotism must all be negated. Of all the people in that wicked city, the one home to which the Saviour chose to invite Himself was that of a despised public official. When the crowd saw the majestic figure of Christ and the tiny tax collector walking side by side into Zacchaeus' home, so well furnished by raiding the treasuries, they said sneeringly: "He has gone in to lodge with one who is a sinner." It is not likely that the mob would ever say that today, because few admit they are sinners. What they would probably say is: "He has gone to the home of that racketeer who was mentioned by the columnists and is about to be convicted by the Grand Jury."

As they converse in secrecy, something happens to the soul of the tax official. Up to this point Zacchaeus was concerned only with whether what he did was "legal"—"Legal" meaning anything is justifiable providing you do not get caught; if you are convicted it means that you violated the law, not that you did what was morally wrong. Zacchaeus shifted his mind from "legality" to "morality," from "being caught" to "doing wrong," from "convention" to "conscience." Where there is wrong there has to be restitution; injustice disturbs the equilibrium of the due order that ought to prevail in society. Giving back the stolen goods restores that balance. Zacchaeus is now ready to make reparation. "Here and now, Lord, I give half of what I have to the poor; and if I have wronged anyone in any way, I make restitution of it fourfold."

Shame is not enough; remorse is not enough; there must also be restitution. As Shakespeare said:

> May one be pardon'd and retain the offence?
>   In the corrupted currents of this world
> Offence's gilded hand may shove by justice,
>   and oft 't is seen the wicked prize itself
> Buys out the law; but 't is not so above;
>   There is no shuffling, there the action lies
> In his true nature, and we ourselves compell'd
>   Even to the teeth and forehead of our faults
> To give in evidence.

Many other crimes are cancelled out by mere sorrow and repentance, but the guilt of robbery, even when dignified with the name of "kickbacks" or "legality," remains, so long as we retain the fruits of it in our own hands. Those who make such restitutions rightly call it "conscience money." A public official who serves ten years in prison for his dishonesty, but all the while keeps the spoils, has not made reparation for his crime either before his country or before his God.

The point of the parable is that honesty in business, honesty among labor unions, honesty in public officials must be based not on "legality" or what they can get away with, but on conscience, that is, giving to every man his due; not because I cannot live away from prison if I am dishonest, but because I cannot live with myself, and I cannot live with myself because I am not living right before my God.

FULTON J. SHEEN
FROM *THOUGHTS FOR DAILY NEEDS*

And Zacchaeus stood, and said unto the Lord; Behold, Lord, the half of my goods I give to the poor; and if I have taken any thing from any man by false accusation, I restore him fourfold. And Jesus said unto him, This day is salvation come to this house, . . . For the Son of man is come to seek and to save that which was lost.
Luke 19:8–10

The Hill Road

There was a man of the Pharisees, named Nicodemus, a ruler of the Jews: The same came to Jesus by night, and said unto him, Rabbi, we know that thou art a teacher come from God: for no man can do these miracles that thou doest, except God be with him. Jesus answered and said unto him, Verily, verily, I say unto thee, Except a man be born again, he cannot see the kingdom of God. Nicodemus saith unto him, How can a man be born when he is old? can he enter the second time into his mother's womb, and be born?

John 3:1–4

od had a song He wanted to sing, and when He had finished it He created a man to sing it. You see, it was a mighty song and needed a Godlike singer. And the man was Jesus, a carpenter of Nazareth. He went up to Jerusalem, and as He walked up and down its narrow, crowded streets, God's song swept across the hearts of people.

Some ran to meet it, it was so full of strength and beauty. But others ran from it, trembling with fear. And these were they who dreaded lest it rend the hate and uproot the falsehood in which their lives were so comfortably grounded.

When the rulers of Israel—priests, scribes, and Pharisees—heard it, they shuttered the windows of their souls and barred the gates of their mind against it; that is, all of them except Nicodemus and one or two others who, when they heard it, stopped to listen.

Nicodemus was no longer a young man, and at first he listened with the gentlemanly indifference of one who is tired of life. But a day came when the swift, clean words cut through the mist of indifference and with a lightning flash revealed Nicodemus to himself. . . .

That night he took the hill road to the Mount of Olives. He had heard that Jesus was in the habit of spending His nights there. . . . The road ended abruptly among a clump of olive trees. . . .

As he stood looking down upon Jerusalem, he felt the presence of long-forgotten memories, and the tall, broad-shouldered dreams of his boyhood seemed to rise from the city of pinnacles and towers lying there so quiet and clean in the white radiance of the Eastern night. Unconsciously he lifted his face toward heaven and stretched out his hands, palms upward, in prayer. In the light of the moon and stars his thin, tired face was like an exquisite cameo of old ivory, carved against the onyx shadows of the olive trees.

Jesus saw him thus. The beauty and pathos of the old man tugged at His heart and quietly, lest He break in upon the prayer, Jesus came and stood beside him. He watched the labored rise and fall of the old man's breathing, the throbbing pulse in the thick veins of his forehead, and at once sensed the courage and endurance it had cost Nicodemus to come out alone and by night up the hill road.

Nicodemus looked up. "You are here. I am so glad." . . .

Now that he was face to face with the young Teacher, Nicodemus was at a loss for words. . . . How could he tell Jesus that for an old man to seek the comradeship of a younger, and for a ruler of Israel, a Hebrew of the Hebrews, a member of the Sanhedrin to have any dealings whatsoever with a Sabbath-breaking Nazarene was not only flagrantly undignified, but dangerously unconventional. But Jesus came to his relief, sensing with instinctive kindliness the older man's difficulty.

"I understand perfectly. It is a bitter experience to be scorned by one's own, an experience from which we may well shrink unless we live so near to God that we are filled with His life."

No sooner had the word *life* been spoken, than Nicodemus found the words for lack of which he had been unable to make his need known. Now he spoke slowly, hesitatingly: "You are a teacher come from God. . . ."

"Are you sure, Nicodemus?" And there was both sadness and a smile in the Master's voice, which Nicodemus was quick to catch.

"You may well ask that. We priests and Pharisees have so often tried to bait you with those very words, but I speak them in all sincerity. Only You can tell me, and my need is too great to be denied—how I, an old man, may find life, *eternal life. . . .*"

Jesus put His hand on that of the old man. "By knowing the God within you, by catching a vision of His Kingdom."

"But it is so long since I have felt God within me—and the eyes of my soul have grown too dim to see so divine a thing as His Kingdom. Surely you realize that I cannot do these things. And if I could—how?"

"There is only one way; you must be born anew."

Nicodemus shook his head and answered with bitter irony: "How can a man be born when he is old? Can he enter his mother's womb over again, and be born?"

"Do not wonder, Nicodemus, at My telling you that you must be born again, spiritually. The wind blows wherever it chooses, and you hear the sound thereof, but you do not know where it comes from or where it goes. This is the way with everyone who owes his birth to the Spirit."

"But how can that be?" Nicodemus asked, bewildered.

"You are a teacher of Israel and yet ignorant of this? I speak of that which I know, and of that which I have seen. You remember how it is told that Moses in the desert lifted the serpent up in the air—even so the Son of Man must be lifted up, so that everyone who believes in Him may have life. Don't you see, Nicodemus? You said your soul seemed to you like a barren, hemmed-in plain. Break down its barriers, widen its horizons, let God's light flood it, and even as the spring sunshine makes the fields blossom, so His light will make your soul alive with new interest, new hope, new joy, new life, life in its fullest sense. Lift up the Son of man within you, and this new life will be life eternal. That's what it means to be born again, Nicodemus, not once, but every day and every hour."

As Jesus spoke these words, night gave place to dawn. The untrammeled song of a lark swept over the hillside and lost itself in the immensity of life waking everywhere.

"It is as though that song had come of my heart," Nicodemus began. He wanted to say more, to make some expression of gratitude, but he could not find the right words. "I came to you in the night," he hesitated, "a soul seemingly without life; now in the dawn I go back—reborn."

ELEANOR B. STOCK

Jesus answered, Verily, verily, I say unto thee, Except a man be born of water and of the Spirit, he cannot enter into the kingdom of God. That which is born of the flesh is flesh; and that which is born of the Spirit is spirit. Marvel not that I said unto thee, Ye must be born again.

John 3:5–7

In the last day, that great day of the feast, Jesus stood and cried, saying, If any man thirst, let him come unto me, and drink. He that believeth on me, as the scripture hath said, out of his belly shall flow rivers of living water. . . . Many of the people therefore, when they heard this saying, said, Of a truth this is the Prophet. Others said, This is the Christ. But some said, Shall Christ come out of Galilee? Hath not the scripture said, That Christ cometh of the seed of David, and out of the town of Bethlehem, where David was? So there was a division among the people because of him. . . . Then answered them the Pharisees, Are ye also deceived? Have any of the rulers or of the Pharisees believed on him? But this people who knoweth not the law are cursed. Nicodemus saith unto them, (he that came to Jesus by night, being one of them,) Doth our law judge any man, before it hear him, and know what he doeth? They answered and said unto him, Art thou also of Galilee? Search, and look: for out of Galilee ariseth no prophet. And every man went unto his own house.

John 7:37, 38, 40–43, 47–53

The painting VISIT OF NICODEMUS TO CHRIST by John La Farge, opposite, portrays the conversation between Nicodemus the Pharisee and Jesus Christ.

Conversion from "Nicodemus"

Nicodemus. Tell me one thing; why do you follow Jesus?

John. It was because of John the Baptist first.

Nicodemus. But why because of him?

John. One day when we were standing by the Jordan, John and my cousin Andrew and myself, we saw a man pass by, tall as a spirit; he did not see us though he passed quite near; indeed we thought it strange; His eyes were open but he looked on nothing; and as he passed, John, pointing with his finger, cried—I can hear him cry it now—"Behold, the Lamb of God!"

Nicodemus. And He, what did He say? What did He do?

John. Nothing; we watched Him slowly climb the hill; His shadow fell before Him; it was evening. Sometimes He stopped to raise His head to the home-flying rooks or greet a countryman with plough on shoulder.

Nicodemus. John said, "Behold, the Lamb of God"?

John. He said so.

Nicodemus. And from that day you followed Him?

John. No, that was afterwards in Galilee.

Nicodemus. But tell me why; why did you follow Him?

John. I think it was our feet that followed Him; it was our feet; our hearts were too afraid. Perhaps indeed it was not in our choice; He tells us that we have not chosen Him, but He has chosen us. I only know that as we followed Him that day He called us we were not walking on the earth at all; it was another world, where everything was new and strange and shining; we pitied men and women at their business, for they knew nothing of what we knew—

Nicodemus. Perhaps it was some miracle He did.

John. It was indeed; more miracles than one; I was not blind and yet He gave me sight; I was not deaf and yet He gave me hearing; Nor was I dead, yet me He raised to life.

ANDREW YOUNG
1885–?

And after that they had mocked him, they took the robe off from him, and put his own raiment on him, and led him away to crucify him. And as they came out, they found a man of Cyrene, Simon by name: him they compelled to bear his cross.
Matthew 27:31, 32

The painting on the opposite page by Ted Hoffman portrays Christ in the garden prior to His arrest and crucifixion on the cross. Simon of Cyrene who helped Jesus carry the cross was probably a Jew coming in from the country to observe Passover in Jerusalem. Tradition has identified Simon of Cyrene with Simeon called Niger of Acts 13:1 who was from Africa.

Simon the Cyrenian Speaks

He never spoke a word to me,
    And yet He called my name;
He never gave a sign to me,
    And yet I knew and came.

At first I said, "I will not bear
    His cross upon my back;
He only seeks to place it there
    Because my skin is black."

But He was dying for a dream,
    And He was very meek,
And in His eyes there shone a gleam
    Men journey far to seek.

It was Himself my pity bought;
    I did for Christ alone
What all of Rome could not have wrought
    With bruise of lash or stone.

COUNTEE CULLEN
1903–1946

Near the Cross

Near the Cross her vigil keeping,
Stood the mother, worn with weeping,
    Where He hung, the dying Lord:
Through her soul, in anguish groaning,
Bowed in sorrow, sighing, moaning,
    Passed the sharp and piercing sword.

O the weight of her affliction!
Hers, who won God's benediction,
    Hers, who bore God's Holy One:
O that speechless, ceaseless yearning!
O those dim eyes never turning
    From her wondrous, suffering Son!

Who upon that mother gazing,
In her trouble so amazing,
    Born of woman, would not weep?
Who of Christ's dear mother thinking,
While her Son that cup is drinking,
    Would not share her sorrow deep?

For His people's sin chastisèd
She beheld her Son despisèd,
    Bound and bleeding 'neath the rod;
Saw the Lord's Anointed taken,
Dying desolate, forsaken,
    Heard Him yield His soul to God.

Near Thy Cross, O Christ, abiding,
Grief and love my heart dividing,
    I with her would take my place:
By Thy guardian Cross uphold me,
In Thy dying, Christ, enfold me
    With the deathless arms of grace.

FROM THE LATIN, 13TH CENTURY;
TR. COMPILED BY LOUIS F. BENSON, 1855–1930

Now there stood by the cross of Jesus his mother, and his mother's sister, Mary the wife of Cleophas, and Mary Magdalene. When Jesus therefore saw his mother, and the disciple standing by, whom he loved, he saith unto his mother, Woman, behold thy son! Then saith he to the disciple, Behold thy mother! And from that hour that disciple took her unto his own home.
John 19:25–27

Jesus was crucified on a hill called Golgotha (a Semitic word meaning skull or place of the skull) outside the gates of Jerusalem. The Romans reserved crucifixion for slaves, thieves, and political prisoners, and this particularly cruel death was imposed upon Roman citizens only for the crime of high treason. Two other men were crucified alongside Jesus; one mocked the dying Jesus, but the other recognized His divinity and asked to be remembered in God's kingdom. The painting opposite by Joseph Maniscalco depicts the agony of the women, especially Jesus' mother, in witnessing this horrible act.

And when they were come unto a place called Golgotha, that is to say, a place of a skull, They gave him vinegar to drink mingled with gall: and when he had tasted thereof, he would not drink. And they crucified him, and parted his garments, casting lots: that it might be fulfilled which was spoken by the prophet, They parted my garments among them, and upon my vesture did they cast lots. And sitting down they watched him there.

Matthew 27:33–36

In fulfillment of the Psalms, "They part my garments among them, and cast lots upon my vesture" (Psalm 22:18), the soldiers cast lots to see which among them would take Jesus' tunic. He suffered six hours on the cross before His life on earth ended. The painting on the opposite page by Peter Bianchi shows a Roman soldier at the moment of Christ's death, when the world turned dark and the earthquake struck.

Gambler

And sitting down, they watched Him there,
The soldiers did;
There, while they played with dice,
He made His sacrifice,
And died upon the Cross to rid
God's world of sin.

He was a gambler, too, my Christ,
He took His life and threw
It for a world redeemed.
And ere His agony was done,
Before the westering sun went down,
Crowning that day with crimson crown,
He knew that He had won.

G. A. STUDDERT-KENNEDY
1883–1929

Upon a Hill

Three men shared death upon a hill,
But only one man died;
The other two—
A thief and God himself—
Made rendezvous.

Three crosses still
Are borne up Calvary's Hill,
Where Sin lifts them high:
Upon the one sag broken men
Who, cursing, die;

Another holds the praying thief,
Or those who, penitent as he,
Still find the Christ
Beside them on the tree.

MIRIAM LeFEVRE CROUSE

Now at that feast he released unto them one prisoner, whomsoever they desired. And there was one named Barabbas, which lay bound with them that had made insurrection with him, who had committed murder in the insurrection. And the multitude crying aloud began to desire him to do as he had ever done unto them. But Pilate answered them, saying, Will ye that I release unto you the King of the Jews? For he knew that the chief priests had delivered him for envy. But the chief priests moved the people, that he should rather release Barabbas unto them. And so Pilate, willing to content the people, released Barabbas unto them, and delivered Jesus, when he had scourged him, to be crucified.

Mark 15:6–11, 15

"The voice of the LORD breaketh the cedars; yea, the LORD breaketh the cedars of Lebanon" (Psalm 29:5). The cedar trees of Lebanon grow up to one-hundred-twenty-five feet tall with branches spread as much as fifty feet, and some trees are believed to have lived more than one thousand years. Knot-free and rot resistant, these great cedars forested the mountain slopes north of Israel and from Old Testament days have come to represent the steadfastness of God and the promise that His love can overcome even the darkest of times.

Good Friday

Am I a stone, and not a sheep,
 That I can stand, O Christ, beneath Thy cross,
 To number drop by drop Thy Blood's slow loss,
And yet not weep?

Not so those women loved
 Who with exceeding grief lamented Thee;
 Not so fallen Peter weeping bitterly;
Not so the thief was moved;

Not so the Sun and Moon
 Which hid their faces in a starless sky.
 A horror of great darkness at broad noon—
I, only I.

Yet give not o'er
 But seek Thy sheep, true Shepherd of the flock;
 Greater than Moses, turn and look once more
And smite a rock.

CHRISTINA ROSSETTI
1830–1894

Barabbas Speaks

I heard a man explaining
(they said his name was Paul)
how Jesus, on that fateful day,
had died to save us all.

I found it hard to follow
His fine-spun theory,
but I am very, very sure
He died that day for me.

EDWIN MCNEILL POTEAT
1892–?

Easter Eve

His murderers met. Their consciences were free:
The sun's eclipse was past, the tumult stilled
In Jewry, and their duty well fulfilled.

Quoth Caiaphas:—
It wrung my heart to see
His mother's grief, God knows. Yet blasphemy
Was proven, the uprising imminent,
And all the church-supporting element
Demanded action, sir, of you and me.

Quoth Pilate:—
When this Nazarene denied
Even Caesar's rule, reluctantly I knew
My duty to the state, sir. Still, I tried,
But found no way, to spare him yet stay true

In loyalty. . . . And still, the poor lad cried,
"Forgive them, for they know not what they do!"

JAMES BRANCH CABELL
1879–1958

Pilate saith unto them, What shall I do then with Jesus which is called Christ? They all say unto him, Let him be crucified. And the governor said, Why, what evil hath he done? But they cried out the more, saying, Let him be crucified. When Pilate saw that he could prevail nothing, but that rather a tumult was made, he took water, and washed his hands before the multitude, saying, I am innocent of the blood of this just person: see ye to it. Then answered all the people, and said, His blood be on us, and on our children.
Matthew 27:22–25

Opposite is a lovely view of a sunset over the Sea of Galilee.

Religious Leaders and Factions

In the second century B.C., Jews in Palestine divided into various religious and political parties, one of the most powerful being the Pharisees, whose name came from a word that means separate. The Pharisees were teachers in the synagogues who diligently studied the scriptures, particularly the strict laws of purity. They followed an intense daily set of rules and religious laws that covered everything from how they ate to how they prayed, and they held themselves apart from the rest of the Jewish community. Jesus disagreed with the Pharisees' emphasis on maintaining the appearance of holiness, and He unmasked their self-righteousness and hypocrisy.

The painting below is entitled THE PHARISEES CONSPIRE TOGETHER, *by James J. Tissot. Declaring that Jesus "not only had broken the sabbath, but said also that God was his father, making himself equal with God" (John 5:18), the Pharisees called for Jesus' arrest and trial as a blasphemer.*

The Pharisees also with the Sadducees came, and tempting desired him that he would shew them a sign from heaven. He answered and said unto them, A wicked and adulterous generation seeketh after a sign; and there shall no sign be given unto it.
Matthew 16:1, 2a, 4a

The Sadducees were the Pharisees' chief rival for religious power. They traced their lineage to the high priests of Solomon's Temple; and their name may have come from Zadok, the high priest from the time of King David. Sadducees based their lives on the books of Moses, Genesis through Deuteronomy. Unlike the Pharisees, they did not believe in an afterlife nor were they interested in the strict rules of purity. The Sadducees enjoyed good relations with Rome, and they worried that Jesus would create a Jewish uprising and bring down the wrath of Rome's rulers. Although they argued with the Pharisees about most issues, the Sadducees agreed that Jesus must be silenced.

The Zealots began in A.D. 6 in response to a census which they believed was the first step toward increased taxation; they became a powerful political party and were uncompromising in their hatred of Rome. During the destruction of Jerusalem by Roman soldiers in A.D. 70, the Zealots became the last holdouts in the stronghold on top of the Masada, a thirteen-hundred-foot high butte overlooking the Dead Sea on which King Herod built a magnificent palace. Here is where more than one thousand men, women, and children chose suicide over surrender; only two women and five children survived. With the fall of Masada, the Romans would not allow the rebuilding of the temple, the Sanhedrin was abolished, the high priesthood came to an end, and the Sadducees ceased to exist.

This relief depicting soldiers parading through Rome with bounty looted from the Temple in Jerusalem is from the Arch of Titus in Rome, a monument built to commemorate the victory of Rome in the first Jewish revolt of A.D. 73. Roman soldiers under Titus, son of the Roman emperor Vespasian, burned and looted the city, crushing all resistance. Rome's victory fulfilled Jesus' prophecy of Matthew 24:2b: "Verily I say unto you, There shall not be left here one stone upon another, that shall not be thrown down."

Pictured below are the ruins of Herod's palace and fortress atop the Masada on the western shore of the Dead Sea. The Masada was only one of many mountaintop fortresses built by Herod the Great; water was provided by a series of deep cisterns fed by an aqueduct that brought water from a dammed wadi. A trail called the Snake Path was the road to the top during the days of Herod; on the opposite side a huge ramp was built by the Roman commander Silva during the siege. In part because of the water supply, the Zealots, who had captured Masada in A.D. 66, were able to hold out for eight years.

Essenes interpreted the religious law in the strictest manner, even more so than the Pharisees; and they lived in isolated communities of self-discipline and self-denial. Essenes believed that a judgment day would come when the Sons of Light would prevail over the Sons of Darkness, destroy life on earth as it existed, and usher in a time of peace and contentment. Their communities clustered in the deserts on the north coast of the Dead Sea, the most celebrated of which was at Qumran, where in the 1940s the Dead Sea Scrolls, written by the Essenes, were discovered.

Pilate Remembers

Do I remember such and such an one?
Nay, Marcus mine, how can I? Every day
The judgment hall was crowded. Every week
A motley throng of victims met their doom.
One Jesus? No. And yet,—and yet,—the name
Does sound familiar. Let me think again—
Jesus from Nazareth in Galilee?
Yes, I recall him now: a strange, still man
With eyes that searched one's very soul, a voice
Of marvelous sweetness, and a face so pure
It scarce seemed human. There again he stands!
All bruised and bleeding, he was dragged in chains
Before the judgment seat. The Jewish priests
Were thirsting for his blood. He claimed, it seems
To be a king; and they had robed him out
In mocking purple, bound his brow with thorns!
Half mad with hate, they gnashed their teeth and cried,
"Away with him. Let him be crucified."
But evidence of legal fault or crime
They could not stablish. Innocent he was
As babe new born. I felt a certain awe
As there with folded hands he stood, and gazed
Right in my eyes, yet gave nor sign nor sound.
He seemed the judge, and I the criminal.
I would have freed him, by the Gods I would,
And strove to do so; but those cursed priests—
Nay, boy, enough, enough. Let memory rest.
Here pass the wine and let us drink to her,
The fair, young slave whom Publius brought from Spain,
Whose queenly grace, and rounded loveliness
Have turned all heads in Rome. Your questions, lad,
Have made me squeamish, turned to sourness
The milk of my content. Let be the past.
I thank the Gods, that two divinities
Have power to lay the peeping ghosts that slip
Through memory's doorway. Thank the Gods, I say,
For wine and women. Fill the cup again!

THOMAS DURLEY LANDELS
1862–?

*Pilate denied responsibility for the decision to crucify Jesus.
In his mind, he had left the choice to the crowd, and they had
determined that Jesus would die on the cross. The painting*
PILATE WASHING HIS HANDS *by Rembrandt Van Rijn depicts
Pilate as he ceremoniously washes his hands of responsibility.*

And Saul, yet breathing out threatenings and slaughter against the disciples of the Lord, went unto the high priest, And desired of him letters to Damascus to the synagogues, that if he found any of this way, whether they were men or women, he might bring them bound unto Jerusalem. And as he journeyed, he came near Damascus: and suddenly there shined round about him a light from heaven: And he fell to the earth, and heard a voice saying unto him, Saul, Saul, why persecutest thou me? And he said, Who art thou, Lord? And the Lord said, I am Jesus whom thou persecutest: it is hard for thee to kick against the pricks. And he trembling and astonished said, Lord, what wilt thou have me to do? And the Lord said unto him, Arise, and go into the city, and it shall be told thee what thou must do. And the men which journeyed with him stood speechless, hearing a voice, but seeing no man. And Saul arose from the earth; and when his eyes were opened, he saw no man: but they led him by the hand, and brought him into Damascus.

Acts 9:1–8

The painting opposite is THE CONVERSION OF ST. PAUL *by Caravaggio. Blinded and humbled on the road to Damascus, Saul was transformed into Paul to become what he called an apostle of Christ Jesus by the will of God.*

The Conversion of St. Paul

The midday sun with fiercest glare,
Broods o'er the hazy, twinkling air;
    Along the level sand
The palm tree's shade unwavering lies,
Just as thy towers, Damascus, rise
    To greet yon wearied band.
The leader of that martial crew
Seems bent some mighty deed to do,
    So steadily he speeds,
With lips firm closed and fixed eye,
Like warrior when the fight is nigh,
    Nor talk nor landscape heeds.
What sudden blaze is round him poured,
As though all heaven's refulgent hoard
    In one rich glory shone?
One moment—and to earth he falls;
What voice his inmost heart appals?
    Voice heard by him alone.
For to the rest both words and form
Seem lost in lightning and in storm,
    While Saul, in wakeful trance,
Sees deep within that dazzling field
His persecuted Lord revealed
    With keen yet pitying glance:
And hears the meek upbraiding call
As gently on his spirit fall
    As if th' Almighty Son
Were prisoner yet in this dark earth,
Nor had proclaimed His royal birth,
    Nor His great power begun.
"Ah, wherefore persecut'st thou me?"
He heard and saw, and sought to free
    His strained eye from the sight;
But heaven's high magic bound it there,
Still gazing, though untaught to bear
    Th' insufferable light.
"Who art Thou, Lord?" he falters forth:
So shall sin ask of heaven and earth
    At the last awful day.
"When did we see Thee suffering nigh,
And passed Thee with unheeding eye?
    Great God of judgment, say?"
Ah! little dream our listless eyes

What glorious presence they despise,
  While in our noon of life,
To power or fame we rudely press,
Christ is at hand, to scorn or bless,
  Christ suffers in our strife.
And though Heaven's gates long since have clos'd,
And our dear Lord in bliss repos'd
  High above mortal ken,
To every ear in every land
(Though meek ears only understand)
  He speaks as He did then.
"Ah! wherefore persecute ye me?
'Tis hard, ye so in love should be
  With your own endless woe.
Know, though at God's right hand I live,
I feel each wound ye reckless give
  To the least saint below.
I in your care My brethren left,
Not willing ye should be bereft
  Of waiting on your Lord.
The meanest offering ye can make—
A drop of water—for love's sake,
  In heaven, be sure, is stor'd."
O by those gentle tones and dear,
When Thou hast stay'd our wild career,
  Thou only hope of souls,
Ne'er let us cast one look behind,
But in the thought of Jesus find
  What every thought controls.
As to Thy last Apostle's heart
Thy lightning glance did then impart
  Zeal's never-dying fire,
So teach us on Thy shrine to lay
Our hearts, and let them day by day
  Intenser blaze and higher.
And as each mild and winning note
(Like pulses that round harp-string's float,
  When the full strain is o'er)
Left lingering on his inward ear
Music, that taught, as death drew near,
  Love's lesson more and more:
So, as we walk our earthly round,
Still may the echo of that sound,
  Be in our memory stor'd:
"Christians! behold your happy state:
Christ is in these, who round you wait;
  Make much of your dear Lord!"

JOHN KEBLE
1792–1866

And there was a certain disciple at Damascus, named Ananias; and to him said the Lord in a vision, Ananias. And he said, Behold, I am here, Lord. And the Lord said unto him, Arise, and go into the street which is called Straight, and enquire in the house of Judas for one called Saul, of Tarsus: for, behold, he prayeth, And hath seen in a vision a man named Ananias coming in, and putting his hand on him, that he might receive his sight. Then Ananias answered, Lord, I have heard by many of this man, how much evil he hath done to thy saints at Jerusalem: And here he hath authority from the chief priests to bind all that call on thy name. But the Lord said unto him, Go thy way: for he is a chosen vessel unto me, to bear my name before the Gentiles, and kings, and the children of Israel: For I will shew him how great things he must suffer for my name's sake.
Acts 9:10–16

On the opposite page are the ruins of Caesarea. The Gospels tell of no visits by Jesus to Caesarea, but the apostles Philip and Peter brought Jesus' message to this Mediterranean city, as did Paul, who embarked from the city on many of his westward travels.

Jesus Gave Them Life

For the most part, the Jews of Jesus' time held to the belief that the day would come when God would send the Messiah, the king of the Jews who would save His people. Prophets of old such as Isaiah and Daniel foretold of this day.

As the trials of Roman occupation weighed increasingly heavy on the Jewish people, they became especially alert for signs of the Messiah, whose coming would signal the beginning of God's Kingdom.

As word of Jesus' miracles of resurrection spread through the land, the faithful took notice. But it was not until Jesus was crucified and rose from the dead that the ancient prophecies were fulfilled and the promise of eternal life given to all men and women of true faith.

A master teacher, Jesus used familiar language and images to help His disciples more fully understand the kingdom of God. Calling them to follow Him, Jesus told the apostles—many of them fishermen who left behind their boats and nets to serve Him—that He would make them "fishers of men." Later, He compared the kingdom of God to "a net, that was cast into the sea, and gathered of every kind: Which, when it was full, they drew to shore, and sat down, and gathered the good into vessels, but cast the bad away" (Matthew 13:47, 48). For men who had lived their lives in a part of the world where fishing was a way of life, such imagery was clear and powerful. At right, a lone fishing boat on the Sea of Galilee.

And, behold, there came a man named Jairus, and he was a ruler of the synagogue: and he fell down at Jesus' feet, and besought him that he would come into his house: For he had one only daughter, about twelve years of age, and she lay a dying. While he yet spake, there cometh one from the ruler of the synagogue's house, saying to him, Thy daughter is dead; trouble not the Master. But when Jesus heard it, he answered him, saying, Fear not: believe only, and she shall be made whole.

Luke 8:41, 42a, 49, 50

The Gospels tell of three times when Jesus raised the dead. He resurrected the widow of Nain's son during a funeral procession (Luke 7:11–18), He brought Lazarus from his tomb back to life (John 11:1–44), and He raised the daughter of Jairus, as depicted opposite in the painting RAISING OF JAIRUS'S DAUGHTER *by Johann Friedrich Overbeck. These three miracles recall three Old Testament miracles of resurrection—two by Elisha and one by Elijah—and they also foreshadow Jesus' own resurrection, which was unique in that, unlike those raised from the dead before Him, Jesus was raised not to continue in His earthly life, but to demonstrate life eternal.*

The Daughter of Jairus

Jesus was at home once more, but He was not permitted to rest. Crowds, larger than He had left, received Him. He was surrounded and overwhelmed. It seemed as if all the invalids in Galilee were moaning after Him. In the heart of His busiest and weariest hour an urgent demand came. . . .

An officer of the Jewish church, an important person, Jairus by name, had a little daughter, dearly cherished. She was scarcely twelve years old, just at the lovely age . . . a winsome maid, her father's darling. She lay at the point of death, and in hot haste messengers had been sent for the Nazarene.

At the feet of Jesus, Jairus flung himself down like a slave, and such an agony went up in his face and attitude as a cold man could not easily have resisted. Jesus, melting with sympathy, tenderly reassured the father, and started at once in the direction of the ruler's house.

But what a throng! When He tried to pass through the people, they closed like a round wall about Him. Such a mass of humanity pressed upon Him that it was impossible to move. At that moment, stealing past the push and rush of the thoughtless throng, a timid hand touched the fringe of his garment, then, terrified, withdrew instantly.

"Who touched me?" Jesus asked quickly. No person in the crowd replied. "Strength goes out of me," insisted the Master. "Who was it?" And the crowd marveled that he even felt it, so great was the press of the multitude.

Jesus and Jairus walked together to the ruler's house. The father did not speak again. He was afraid of offending the rabbi. After those first hot words, the first wild moment, what could he do? When the servant came, weeping, and told him that it was too late, not to trouble the Master, for the little maid was gone—his heart had broken in one mad outcry. This great Healer, this mysterious man, so famous for His tenderness, so marvelous for His pity, must needs fail him, him, Jairus, out of all Palestine, and that in the hour of his terrible need! For the fact could not be denied that Jesus had stopped on the way to a dying patient to cure an old, chronic case. That woman could have been healed just as well tonight, tomorrow, or next week. But He had lingered. And the child was dead.

"Do not be afraid," said Jesus, tenderly; "only believe!" But His face was very grave. And by a single motion of His expressive hand He ordered all His disciples back but three—Peter, James, and John, His dearest. The group entered the ruler's house. The house was not silent. . . . Obtrusive wails and groans, mingled with genuine sobs and tears, filled the place. Jesus seemed surprised at the condition in which He found the family.

"The child is not dead," He said, decidedly. Some of the neighbors, who did not altogether believe in the famous Healer, began to laugh. It was a derisive laugh, a cold sound in that house of woe, and it did not please Him. A keen rebuke shot from His mild eyes at the unseemly scorn. "Nay," He repeated, "she is not dead. She is asleep."

He spoke in the tone of a man who was not to be gainsaid. . . . He went into the sick room and looked at the child. "This is sleep," he persisted. . . . The father's sobs had ceased. The mother lifted her face, discolored with tears, worn with watching, and piteously raised her hands. The three friends of the rabbi stood reverently wondering.

Jesus silently regarded the little maid. She lay unconscious and was quite rigid. Jesus looked at her with a strange expression. His eyes seemed to say: "It is between Me and thee, little maid. We understand." . . .

Now He looked at the little girl with the tenderness that is only to be expected of those in whom the love of children is profound and genuine. She seemed to quiver beneath His look, but her color and her attitude did not change. Then He took her by the hand.

Her little wasted fingers lay for a few moments in His . . . vital grasp; then He felt them tremble. . . . Who sees the instant when the lily blossoms? Who could have detected the moment of time in which the child began to stir? Was it His hand that moved, or hers that directed His slowly upward till it reached her pillow, and so came upon a level with her face?

It did not seem sudden or startling, but only the most natural thing in the world, when the little girl laid her cheek upon His palm.

ELIZABETH STUART PHELPS
FROM *THE STORY OF JESUS CHRIST*

And when he came into the house, he suffered no man to go in, save Peter, and James, and John, and the father and the mother of the maiden And all wept, and bewailed her: but he said, Weep not; she is not dead, but sleepeth. And they laughed him to scorn, knowing that she was dead. And he put them all out, and took her by the hand, and called, saying, Maid, arise. And her spirit came again, and she arose straightway.
Luke 8:51–55a

Now a certain man was sick, named Lazarus, of Bethany, the town of Mary and her sister Martha. Therefore his sisters sent unto him, saying, Lord, behold, he whom thou lovest is sick. When Jesus heard that, he said, This sickness is not unto death, but for the glory of God, that the Son of God might be glorified thereby. Now Jesus loved Martha, and her sister, and Lazarus. When he had heard therefore that he was sick, he abode two days still in the same place where he was. And after that he saith unto them, Our friend Lazarus sleepeth; but I go, that I may awake him out of sleep. Then said his disciples, Lord, if he sleep, he shall do well. Howbeit Jesus spake of his death: but they thought that he had spoken of taking of rest in sleep. Then said Jesus unto them plainly, Lazarus is dead. And I am glad for your sakes that I was not there, to the intent ye may believe; nevertheless let us go unto him. Then said Thomas, which is called Didymus, unto his fellowdisciples, Let us also go, that we may die with him.

John 11:1, 3–6, 11b–16

Lazarus and Mary

Now as Christ
Drew near to Bethany, the Jews went forth
With Martha mourning Lazarus. But Mary
Sat in the house. She knew the hour was nigh
When He would go again, as He had said,
Unto his Father; and she felt that He,
Who loved her brother Lazarus in Life,
Had chose the hour to bring him home thro' Death
In no unkind forgetfulness. Alone—
She could lift up the bitter pray to heaven,
"Thy will be done, O God!" But once more
Came Martha, saying, "Lo, the Lord is here
And calleth for thee, Mary!" Then arose
The mourner from the ground, whereon she sat
Shrouded in sackcloth, and bound quickly up
The golden locks of her dishevel'd hair,
And o'er her ashy garments drew a veil
Hiding the eyes she could not trust. And still,
As she made ready to go forth, a calm
As in a dream fell on her.
    At a fount
Hard by the sepulchre, without the wall,
Jesus awaited Mary. Seated near
Were the way-worn disciples in the shade;
But, of himself forgetful, Jesus lean'd
Upon his staff, and watch'd where she should come,
To whose one sorrow—but a sparrow's falling—
The pity that redeem'd a world could bleed!
And as she came, with that uncertain step,—
Eager, yet weak, her hands upon her breast,—
And they who follow'd her all fallen back
To leave her with her sacred grief alone,—
The heart of Christ was troubled. She drew near;
Then, with a vain strife to control her tears,
She stagger'd to the midst, and at His feet
Fell prostrate, saying, "Lord! hadst thou been here,
My brother had not died!" The Saviour groan'd
In spirit, and stoop'd tenderly, and raised
The mourner from the ground, and in a voice
Broke in its utterance like her own, He said,
"Where have ye laid him?" Then the Jews who came
Following Mary, answer'd through their tears
"Lord, come and see!" But lo! the mighty heart
That in Gethsemane sweat drops of blood,

Taking from us the cup that might not pass—
The heart whose breaking cord upon the cross
Made the earth tremble, and the sun afraid
To look upon his agony—the heart
Of a lost world's Redeemer—overflowed,
Touched by a mourner's sorrow! Jesus wept.
Calm'd by those pitying tears, and fondly brooding
Upon the thought that Christ so loved her brother,
Stood Mary there; but that lost burden now
Lay on His heart who pitied her; and Christ,
Following slow and groaning in Himself,
Came to the sepulchre. It was a cave,
And a stone lay upon it. Jesus said,
"Take ye away the stone!" Then lifted He
His moisten'd eyes to heaven, and while the Jews
And the disciples bent their heads in awe,
And, trembling, Mary sank upon her knees,
The Son of God pray'd audibly. He ceased,
And for a minute's space there was a hush,
As if th' angelic watchers of the world
Had stayed the pulse of all breathing things,
To listen to that prayer. The face of Christ
Shone as he stood, and over Him there came
Command as 'twere the living face of God,
And with a loud voice, he cried, "Lazarus!
Come forth!" And instantly, bound hand and foot,
And borne by unseen angels from the cave,
He that was dead stood with them. At the word
Of Jesus, the fear-stricken Jews unloosed
The bands from off the foldings of his shroud;
And Mary, with her dark veil thrown aside,
Ran to him swiftly, and cried, "Lazarus!
My brother Lazarus!" and tore away
The napkin she had bound about his head—
And touched the warm lips with her fearful hand—
And on his neck fell weeping.

NATHANIEL PARKER WILLIS
1806–1867

Then when Jesus came, he found that he had lain in the grave four days already. And many of the Jews came to Martha and Mary, to comfort them concerning their brother. Then Martha, as soon as she heard that Jesus was coming, went and met him: . . . Then said Martha unto Jesus, Lord, if thou hadst been here, my brother had not died. But I know, that even now, whatsoever thou wilt ask of God, God will give it thee. Jesus saith unto her, Thy brother shall rise again. Martha saith unto him, I know that he shall rise again in the resurrection at the last day. Jesus said unto her, I am the resurrection, and the life: he that believeth in me, though he were dead, yet shall he live.
John 11:17, 19–25

The Touch of the Master's Hand

'Twas battered and scarred, and the auctioneer
Thought it scarcely worth his while
To waste much time on the old violin,
But held it up with a smile.
"What am I bidden, good folks," he cried,
"Who'll start the bidding for me?"
"A dollar, a dollar"; then "Two! Only two?
Two dollars, who'll make it three?
Three dollars, once; three dollars, twice;
Going for three—" But no,
From the room, far back, a gray-haired man
Came forward and picked up the bow;
Then, wiping the dust from the old violin,
And tightening the loose strings,
He played a melody pure and sweet
As a caroling angel sings.

The music ceased, and the auctioneer,
With a voice that was quiet and low,
Said: "What am I bid for the old violin?"
And he held it up with the bow.
"A thousand dollars, and who'll make it two?
Two thousand! And who'll make it three?
Three thousand, once; three thousand, twice,
And going, and gone," said he.
The people cheered, but some of them cried,
"We do not quite understand
What changed its worth." Swift came the reply:
"The touch of a master's hand."

And many a man with life out of tune,
And battered and scarred with sin,
Is auctioned cheap to the thoughtless crowd,
Much like the old violin.
A "mess of pottage," a glass of wine;
A game—and he travels on.
He is "going" once, and "going" twice,
He's "going" and almost "gone."
But the Master comes, and the foolish crowd
Never can quite understand
The worth of a soul and the change that's wrought
By the touch of the Master's hand.

MYRA BROOKS WELCH
?–1959

When Jesus therefore saw her weeping, and the Jews also weeping which came with her, he groaned in the spirit, and was troubled, And said, Where have ye laid him? They said unto him, Lord, come and see. Jesus wept. Then said the Jews, Behold how he loved him! Jesus therefore again groaning in himself cometh to the grave. It was a cave, and a stone lay upon it. Jesus said, Take ye away the stone. Then they took away the stone from the place where the dead was laid. And Jesus . . . cried with a loud voice, Lazarus, come forth. And he that was dead came forth.
John 11:33–36, 38, 39a, 41, 43b, 44a

When Lazarus died, Jesus was in Perea, east of Jerusalem. He had traveled there for a brief retreat after a year of preaching in Jerusalem, where the Sanhedrin had begun to conspire against Him. When Martha and Mary sent for Jesus, He knew that danger awaited Him in Jerusalem, yet He went. Although Lazarus had been dead four days, Jesus brought him back to life. The miracle aroused the people of Jerusalem, both those who believed in Jesus and those who sought to stop His teaching. The furor over the raising of Lazarus helped force the confrontation between Jesus and the Sanhedrin to its final climax. The painting opposite is THE RESURRECTION OF LAZARUS by the artist Jean-Baptiste Corneille.

But Mary stood without at the sepulchre weeping: and as she wept, she stooped down, and looked into the sepulchre, And seeth two angels in white sitting, the one at the head, and the other at the feet, where the body of Jesus had lain. And they say unto her, Woman, why weepest thou? She saith unto them, Because they have taken away my Lord, and I know not where they have laid him. And when she had thus said, she turned herself back, and saw Jesus standing, and knew not that it was Jesus.

John 20:11–14

Mary Magdalene

 t was in the month of June when I saw Him for the first time. He was walking in the wheatfield when I passed by with my handmaidens, and He was alone.

The rhythm of His step was different from other men's, and the movement of His body was like naught I had seen before. Men do not pace the earth in that manner. And even now I do not know whether He walked fast or slow.

My handmaidens pointed their fingers at Him and spoke in shy whispers to one another. And I stayed my steps for a moment, and raised my hand to hail Him. But He did not turn His face, and He did not look at me. . . . I was swept back into myself, and I was as cold as if I had been in a snow-drift. And I shivered.

That night I beheld Him in my dreaming; and they told me afterward that I screamed in my sleep and was restless upon my bed.

It was in the month of August that I saw Him again, through my window. He was sitting in the shadow of the cypress tree across my garden, and He was as still as if He had been carved out of stone, . . . And my slave, the Egyptian, came to me and said, "That man is here again. He is sitting there across your garden."

And I gazed at Him, and my soul quivered within me, for He was beautiful. . . . Then I clothed myself with raiment of Damascus, and I left my house and walked towards Him. . . . Was it hunger in my eyes that desired comeliness, or was it His beauty that sought the light of my eyes? Even now I do not know.

I walked to Him with my scented garments and my golden sandals . . . and when I reached him, I said, "Good-morrow to you."

And He said, "Good-morrow to you, Miriam."

And He looked at me, and His night-eyes saw me as no man had seen me. And suddenly I was as if naked, and I was shy. Yet He had said only, "Good-morrow to you."

And then I said to Him, "Will you not come to my house? . . . Will you not have wine and bread with me?"

And He said, "Yes, Miriam, but not now."

Not now, not now, He said. And the voice of the sea was in those two words and the voice of the wind and the trees. And when He said them unto me, life spoke to death.

For mind you, my friend, I was dead. I was a woman who had divorced her soul. I was living apart from this self which you now see. I belonged to all men, and to none. They called me harlot, and a woman possessed of seven devils. I was cursed, and I was envied.

But when His dawn-eyes looked into my eyes all the stars of my night faded away, and I became Miriam, only Miriam, a woman lost to the earth she had known, and finding herself in new places.

And now again I said to Him, "Come into my house and share bread and wine with me."

And He said, "Why do you bid me to be your guest?"

And I said, "I beg you to come into my house." And it was all that was sod in me, and all that was sky in me, calling unto Him.

Then He looked at me, and the noontide of His eyes was upon me, and He said, "You have many lovers, and yet I alone love you. Other men love themselves in your nearness. I love you in yourself. Other men see a beauty in you that shall fade away sooner than their own years. But I see in you a beauty that shall not fade away, and in the autumn of your days that beauty shall not be afraid to gaze at itself in the mirror, and it shall not be offended. I alone love the unseen in you."

Then He said in a low voice: "Go away now. If this cypress tree is yours and you would not have me sit in its shadow, I will walk my way."

And I cried to Him and I said: "Master, come to my house. I have incense to burn for you, and a silver basin for your feet. You are a stranger, and yet not a stranger. I entreat you, come to my house."

Then He stood up and looked at me even as the seasons might look down upon the field, and He smiled. And He said again: "All men love you for themselves. I love you for yourself."

And then He walked away. But no other man ever walked the way He walked. Was it a breath born in my garden that moved to the east? Or was it a storm that would shake all things to their foundations?

I knew not, but on that day the sunset of His eyes slew the dragon in me, and I became a woman, I became Miriam, Miriam of Migdel.

KAHLIL GIBRAN
FROM *JESUS THE SON OF MAN*

Jesus saith unto her, Woman, why weepest thou? whom seekest thou? She, supposing him to be the gardener, saith unto him, Sir, if thou have borne him hence, tell me where thou hast laid him, and I will take him away. Jesus saith unto her, Mary. She turned herself, and saith unto him, Rabboni; which is to say, Master. Jesus saith unto her, Touch me not; for I am not yet ascended to my Father: but go to my brethren, and say unto them, I ascend unto my Father, and your Father; and to my God, and your God. Mary Magdalene came and told the disciples that she had seen the Lord, and that he had spoken these things unto her.

John 20:15–18

A Guard of the Sepulcher

I was a Roman soldier in my prime;
Now age is on me and the yoke of time.
I saw your Risen Christ, for I am he
Who reached the hyssop to Him on the tree;
And I am one of two who watched beside
The Sepulcher of Him we crucified.
All that last night I watched with sleepless eyes;
Great stars arose and crept across the skies.
The world was all too still for mortal rest,
For pitiless thoughts were busy in the breast.
The night was long, so long, it seemed at last
I had grown old and a long life had passed.
Far off, the hills of Moab, touched with light,
Were swimming in the hollow of the night.
I saw Jerusalem all wrapped in cloud
Stretched like a dead thing folded in a shroud.
Once in the pauses of our whispered talk
I heard a something on the garden walk.
Perhaps it was a crisp leaf lightly stirred—
Perhaps the dream-note of a waking bird.
Then suddenly an angel burning white
Came down with earthquake in the breaking light,
And rolled the great stone from the Sepulcher,
Mixing the morning with a scent of myrrh.
And, lo, the Dead had risen with the day:
The Man of Mystery had gone His way.

    Years have I wandered, carrying my shame;
Now let the tooth of time eat out my name.
For we, who all the wonder might have told,
Kept silence, for our mouths were stopt with gold.

EDWIN MARKHAM
1852–1940

Now the next day, that followed the day of the preparation, the chief priests and Pharisees came together unto Pilate, Saying, Sir, we remember that that deceiver said, while he was yet alive, After three days I will rise again. Command therefore that the sepulchre be made sure until the third day, lest his disciples come by night, and steal him away, and say unto the people, He is risen from the dead: so the last error shall be worse than the first. Pilate said unto them, Ye have a watch: go your way, make it as sure as ye can. So they went, and made the sepulchre sure, sealing the stone, and setting a watch.
Matthew 27:62–66

The Gospels tell us that, after the crucifixion, Joseph of Arimathaea took possession of Jesus' body, prepared it for burial, and brought it to a tomb near Golgotha. Some scholars speculate that Joseph may have been a member of the Sanhedrin, secretly devoted to Jesus, who risked his own life by asking Pilate for Christ's body; the Gospel of John calls him a "disciple of Jesus, but secretly." (John 19:38). The traditional site of Jesus' tomb is located within the modern city of Jerusalem and marked by the Church of the Holy Sepulchre. The tomb in which Christ's body was laid probably looked much like the one opposite, located in a garden in modern Jerusalem.

But Thomas, one of the twelve, . . . was not with them when Jesus came. The other disciples therefore said unto him, We have seen the Lord. But he said unto them, Except I shall see in his hands the print of the nails, and put my finger into the print of the nails, and thrust my hand into his side, I will not believe. And . . . then came Jesus, the doors being shut, and stood in the midst, and said, Peace be unto you. Then saith he to Thomas, Reach hither thy finger, and behold my hands; and reach hither thy hand, and thrust it into my side: and be not faithless, but believing. And Thomas answered and said unto him, My Lord and my God. Jesus saith unto him, Thomas, because thou hast seen me, thou hast believed: blessed are they that have not seen, and yet have believed.

John 20:24–29

Thomas is often remembered as the doubter among Jesus' apostles, yet there is more to Thomas than doubt alone. When Jesus tells His disciples that He is going to Jerusalem to seek out Lazarus, despite the fact that danger awaits Him there, all but Thomas urge Him not to go. Thomas declares they should not prevent Jesus from going, but rather go with Him. This is not a man plagued by doubt, but a man guided by devotion to His Master. Opposite, in a painting by Leslie Benson, Thomas reaches to touch Jesus' wounds after His resurrection.

Unbelieving Thomas

There was a seal upon the stone,
A guard around the tomb:
The spurned and trembling band alone
Bewail their Master's doom.
They deemed the barriers of the grave
Had closed o'er Him who came to save;
And thoughts of grief and gloom
Were darkening, while depressed, dismayed,
Silent they wept, or weeping prayed.
  He died;—for justice claimed her due,
  Ere guilt could be forgiven:
But soon the gates asunder flew,
The iron bands were riven;
Broken the seal; the guards dispersed,
Upon their sight in glory burst
The risen Lord of Heaven!
Yet one, the heaviest in despair,
In grief the wildest was not there.
  Returning, on each altered brow
With mute surprise he gazed,
For each was lit with transport now,
Each eye to heaven upraised.
Burst forth from each th' ecstatic word—
"Hail, brother, we have seen the Lord!"
Bewildered and amazed
He stood; then bitter words and brief
Betrayed the heart of unbelief.
  Days passed, and still the frequent groan
  Convulsed his laboring breast;
When round him light celestial shone,
And Jesus stood confessed.
"Reach, doubter! reach thy hand," he said;
"Explore the wound the spear hath made,
The front by nails impressed:
No longer for the living grieve,
And be not faithless, but believe."
  Oh! if the iris of the skies
  Transcends the painter's art,
How could he trace to human eyes
The rainbow of the heart;
When love, joy, fear, repentance, shame,
Hope, faith, in swift succession came,
Each claiming there a part;
Each mingling in the tears that flowed,
The words that breathed—"My Lord! My God!"

THOMAS DALE
1797–1870

On the Road to Emmaus

And, behold, two of them went that same day to a village called Emmaus, which was from Jerusalem about threescore furlongs. And they talked together of all these things which had happened. And it came to pass, that, while they communed together and reasoned, Jesus himself drew near, and went with them. But their eyes were holden that they should not know him. And he said unto them, What manner of communications are these that ye have one to another, as ye walk, and are sad? And the one of them, whose name was Cleopas, answering said unto him, Art thou only a stranger in Jerusalem, and hast not known the things which are come to pass there in these days?

Luke 24:13–18

It was one of those evenings when every tree seems to have been dipped in crystal, and the scarlet anemones on the hills glowed like molten rubies. In the cool greenish light of evening the furrowed earth looked softly pale. . . .

Nathanael and Cleopas had set out from Jerusalem in the forenoon; now their shadows were lengthening. During the journey they exchanged few words between them, until they came close to Emmaus. Then, when it was growing darker, and their spirits were oppressed by the memories that crowded on them with the coming of night, they spoke more often, with long silences between.

"Is he alive or dead—that's the question!" Cleopas said sharply, planting his staff firmly on the ground. "If he is alive, where is he? And if he is dead, what have the tomb-robbers done to him? Well, I saw the empty tomb! How do you explain it, Nathanael?"

"Did not the woman say she saw him?" Nathanael said after a pause.

"Yes, she did. She said there was a gardener standing in the garden, and wearing a hat to shade his face, and she knew he was Jesus. But when I asked her to describe him—whether there were wounds on his hands and feet, and whether there was blood on his forehead from the crown of thorns, and what clothes he was wearing, why, she answered nothing at all. Well, I believe the rats ate up his flesh, or the tomb broke open in the thunderstorm, or the grave-robbers found him! As for the story of the angel sitting on the tomb—why, that's an old wives' tale. It was a fool's journey, and we were fools to follow him! I shall have no sleep at night, thinking of the trick he has played upon us! You have your faith, but as for me, I won't believe he is alive until I see him with my own eyes."

"Then what will you do?"

"I will do what all men do when they see a friend who has returned. I shall run into his arms with such joy that the sound of my cry will be heard for a hundred miles! I loved him with all my heart, but loving a dead man is something else altogether. Didn't he say: 'Let the dead bury the dead'? Well, let the dead Christ bury the dead Christ!"

With these words Cleopas shook his head, fell into a long silence, and said nothing more until the walls of Emmaus came in sight. The small white-walled village lay in a hollow among vineyards and fruit trees. It was set a little way from the Roman road, and was reached through the grove of walnuts. The two men were halfway through the walnut grove when they heard footsteps behind them. Nathanael looked over his shoulder, but there was no one in sight. Probably the man, whoever he was, was hidden by the walnut trees, or it might be someone walking within the town. It had been a strange afternoon, with a lowering sky and the threat of a storm; they were glad to be close to the village, for the strangeness and emptiness of the evening frightened them. The wind was rising, and a thick white dust came through the trees.

The sound of footsteps grew louder, and soon they became aware that someone else was walking near them. There were three long bluish shadows on the dusty road between the walnut trees. They turned and saw a man of middle height, who wore the costume of a Passover pilgrim, and to judge by the blue tassels on the edge of his cloak, he was a rabbi or a scribe. His gown was covered with dust, and to keep the dust from his mouth and nostrils he wore a scarf over the lower part of his face, and he concealed his hands within the folds of his cloak. They saw only the deep smoldering eyes, and they could barely guess at the shape of his face.

The man must have heard the muttering of Cleopas, for he said: "Why are you so sad, brother?"

"We are all sad these days," Cleopas answered. "Who can be happy now that Jesus is dead?"

"Look upon me," said the stranger quietly. "Surely you know me?" he insisted.

"I see you are a rabbi and a learned man, but you have a rag across your mouth—"

"Surely you know my voice?"

"There are many who speak like you. Forgive me, I do not remember everyone I have seen."

"Look upon me," the stranger repeated, and his hand tore away the scarf covering his mouth.

He looked at the stranger, but it was too dark for him to see the man's features clearly. The hand was wet with blood, but it meant nothing to him, for the stranger might have scratched it on a thorn tree.

"Surely you know me!" the stranger said. "Have we journeyed together all these years in vain? I plucked you, Cleopas, from the fields one day when you were sick unto death, and you, Nathanael, I plucked you from under a fig tree. Do you not know me?"

"Yes, we know you," Cleopas answered, but he spoke like a man who did not know.

In silence they walked into Emmaus. Night had settled on the walled village and the heavens were streaming with stars. They walked through the shadowy streets like sleepwalkers, and when they came to an inn Nathanael said: "Abide with us, for it is late and the day is far spent, and let us feast as we feasted in days gone by."

And still Nathanael did not believe that Jesus was at his side. He would glance at the stranger, who was very pale and curiously withdrawn, speaking in an unrecognizable voice, his eyes glowing like coals which have been blown upon. It was perhaps some messenger of Jesus, or a brother, or even a distant relative. Nathanael felt no alarm at the stranger's presence. Often during his journeys some stranger would accost him, talk for a while and then vanish on his own errands. What puzzled him more than anything else was the unnatural stillness which had descended upon the village. At this hour of the evening you expected to hear a great number of distinct sounds—caravans unloading for the night, women singing at the fountain, the cracking of whips, drunken voices. But even the birds which usually sang in the evening sky were silent.

ROBERT PAYNE
FROM *THE LORD JESUS*

And they drew nigh unto the village, whither they went: and he made as though he would have gone further. But they constrained him, saying, Abide with us: for it is toward evening, and the day is far spent. And he went in to tarry with them. And it came to pass, as he sat at meat with them, he took bread, and blessed it, and brake, and gave to them. And their eyes were opened, and they knew him; and he vanished out of their sight. And they said one to another, Did not our heart burn within us, while he talked with us by the way, and while he opened to us the scriptures? And they rose up the same hour, and returned to Jerusalem, and found the eleven gathered together, and them that were with them, Saying, The Lord is risen indeed, and hath appeared to Simon.
Luke 24:28–34

The Walk to Emmaus

It happened, on a solemn eventide,
Soon after he that was our surety died,
Two bosom friends, each pensively inclined,
The scene of all those sorrows left behind,
Sought their own village, busied, as they went,
In musings worthy of the great event:
They spake of him they loved, of him whose life,
Though blameless, had incurred perpetual strife
Whose deeds had left, in spite of hostile arts,
A deep memorial graven on their hearts.
The recollection, like a vein of ore,
The farther traced, enriched them still the more;
They thought him, and they justly thought him, one
Sent to do more than He appeared t' have done;
To exalt a people, and to place them high
Above all else, and wondered he should die.
Ere yet they brought their journey to an end,
A Stranger joined them, courteous as a friend,
And asked them, with a kind engaging air,
What their affliction was, and begged a share.
Informed, he gathered up the broken thread,
And, truth and wisdom gracing all he said,
Explained, illustrated, and searched so well,
The tender theme, on which they chose to dwell,
That reaching home, "The night," they said, "is near,
We must not now be parted, sojourn here."
The new acquaintance soon became a guest,
And, made so welcome at their simple feast,
He blessed the bread, but vanished at the word,
And left them both exclaiming, "'Twas the Lord!
Did not our hearts feel all he deigned to say,
Did they not burn within us by the way?"

WILLIAM COWPER
1731–1800

The painting at left is THE SUPPER AT EMMAUS *by Caravaggio. Some scholars believe the city Nicopolis, northwest of Jerusalem, is the modern location of the town of Emmaus. The word* Emmaus *comes from a root word meaning warm water, and within Nicopolis are two wells known for their lukewarm water.*

The End of Life

The Hebrew word *Sheol* described the region below the earth to which all souls descended after death. To the Old Testament faithful, it represented neither punishment nor reward, but was simply a powerless, unconscious state of being. The prospect of passing into Sheol was frightful to most ancient Hebrews, since all knowledge and consciousness of their God would be gone once their earthly lives ended. Jesus provided a release from this fear of death, however, when He rose from the grave. Through His physical resurrection, He offered the hope of salvation and everlasting life to all those who believed in Him.

> *But is now made manifest by the appearing*
> *of our Saviour Jesus Christ,*
> *who hath abolished death,*
> *and hath brought life and immortality*
> *to light through the gospel.*
> *II Timothy 1:10*

Below, the exterior of Old Testament tombs stands as a reminder of ancient Israel.

Death was ever-present in biblical Judea, and the Jews had strict rules for handling the dead. Fifty percent of the people did not live to the age of eighteen. Anyone who touched a corpse was considered unclean for seven days, and required to undergo ritualistic washing on the third and seventh days. Priests were allowed near the corpses only of their own family members. Jesus taught a distinction between physical impurity, such as that which came from unwashed hands, and moral impurity, which was of greater concern.

Ancient Jews expressed grief not only with crying, but also in wailing and the tearing of clothes. If the deceased were especially important to the mourners, they wore sackcloth to symbolize grief. Other traditional rituals included rolling in dust and removing head coverings. The wealthy often hired mourning women to follow the funeral procession and wail in the traditional manner.

Whatsoever thy hand findeth to do,
do it with thy might:
for there is no work, nor device,
nor knowledge, nor wisdom,
in the grave, whither thou goest.
Ecclesiastes 9:10

For out of the heart proceed
evil thoughts, murders, adulteries,
fornications, thefts, false witness,
blasphemies: These are the things
which defile a man:
but to eat with unwashen hands
defileth not a man.
Matthew 15:19, 20

The Jews did not embalm their dead; but generally washed, wrapped, and buried or entombed the body within twenty-four hours. Proper burial displayed respect for the dead. Those without money to own a private tomb covered the bodies of their loved ones with stones or lay them in public grave sites. The wealthy had many-chambered family tombs built into the cliffs and caves outside the city limits. Here the body was covered with a shroud, placed on a bier, and carried to the tomb where it was laid on a stone ledge. Eventually, each body was removed to a deeper chamber within the tomb, where it could lie forever with its ancestors and descendants.

At left, the interior of the tomb of the kings of Israel in Jerusalem. The tombs date from about the seventh century B.C. During this period, it was forbidden to all but kings to be buried inside the city walls.

Feed My Lambs

But when the morning was now come, Jesus stood on the shore: but the disciples knew not that it was Jesus. Then Jesus saith unto them, Children, have ye any meat? They answered him, No.

And he said unto them, Cast the net on the right side of the ship, and ye shall find.

They cast therefore, and now they were not able to draw it for the multitude of fishes. Therefore that disciple whom Jesus loved saith unto Peter, It is the Lord.

Now when Simon Peter heard that it was the Lord, he girt his fisher's coat unto him, (for he was naked,) and did cast himself into the sea. And the other disciples came in a little ship; (for they were not far from land, but as it were two hundred cubits,) dragging the net with fishes. As soon then as they were come to land, they saw a fire of coals there, and fish laid thereon, and bread.

Jesus saith unto them, Bring of the fish which ye have now caught.

Simon Peter went up, and drew the net to land full of great fishes, an hundred and fifty and three: and for all there were so many, yet was not the net broken. Jesus saith unto them, Come and dine. And none of the disciples durst ask him, Who art thou? knowing that it was the Lord.

Jesus then cometh, and taketh bread, and giveth them, and fish likewise. This is now the third time that Jesus shewed himself to his disciples, after that he was risen from the dead.

So when they had dined, Jesus saith to Simon Peter, Simon, son of Jonas, lovest thou me more than these?

He saith unto him, Yea, Lord; thou knowest that I love thee.

He saith unto him, Feed my lambs.

He saith to him again the second time, Simon, son of Jonas, lovest thou me?

He saith unto him, Yea, Lord; thou knowest that I love thee.

He saith unto him, Feed my sheep.

He saith unto him the third time, Simon, son of Jonas, lovest thou me?

Peter was grieved because he said unto him the third time, Lovest thou me? And he said unto him, Lord, thou knowest all things; thou knowest that I love thee.

Jesus saith unto him, Feed my sheep.

JOHN 21:4–17

Then the eleven disciples went away into Galilee, into a mountain where Jesus had appointed them. And when they saw him, they worshipped him: but some doubted. And Jesus came and spake unto them, saying, All power is given unto me in heaven and in earth. Go ye therefore, and teach all nations, baptizing them in the name of the Father, and of the Son, and of the Holy Ghost: Teaching them to observe all things whatsoever I have commanded you: and, lo, I am with you alway, even unto the end of the world. Amen.
Matthew 28:16–20

The painting on the opposite page by an unknown artist portrays the compassion of the resurrected Christ as He seeks out His followers. In providing food that satisfied His disciples' physical hunger, Jesus not only demonstrated His love for them but also His command to "Feed my sheep" with the food of the spirit: the saving gospel of Christ Jesus.

How He Came

When the golden evening gathered
on the shore of Galilee,
When the fishing boats lay quiet by the sea,
Long ago the people wondered,
tho' no sign was in the sky,
For the glory of the Lord was passing by.

Not in robes of purple splendor,
not in silken softness shod,
But in raiment worn with travel came their God,
And the people knew His presence
by the heart that ceased to sigh
When the glory of the Lord was passing by.

For He healed their sick at even,
and He cured the leper's sore,
And sinful men and women sinned no more,
And the world grew mirthful-hearted,
and forgot its misery
When the glory of the Lord was passing by.

Not in robes of purple splendor,
but in lives that do His will,
In patient acts of kindness He comes still;
And the people cry with wonder,
tho' no sign is in the sky,
That the glory of the Lord is passing by.

W. J. DAWSON
1854–1928

A spectacular sunset over the Sea of Galilee.

Places Where Jesus Touched Lives

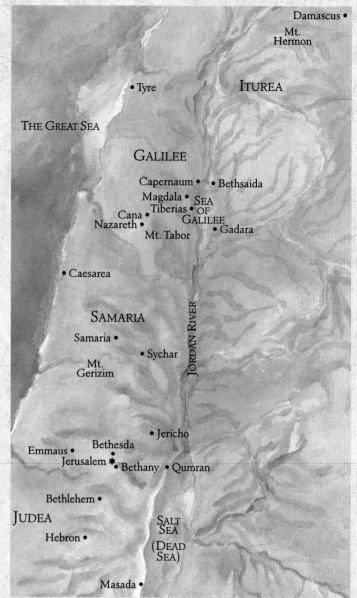

BETHANY. The home of Mary, Martha, and Lazarus, Bethany was a small settlement about one and one-half miles outside of Jerusalem on a hill leading to the Mount of Olives. Between Bethany and Jerusalem, Jesus caused the fig tree to wither.

BETHESDA. The pools of Bethesda, where Jesus healed the lame man, were just outside the triumphal arch of Jerusalem, but outside the town proper. Here the Romans built a temple to Aesculapius, god of medicine; remains of the temple now lie in the center of the pools and partially under a Byzantine church.

BETHSAIDA. This fishing community located on the Sea of Galilee was the home of Philip, Andrew, and Peter.

CANA. About ten miles northeast of Nazareth, Cana was the site of Jesus' first miracle at the wedding feast.

CAPERNAUM. A fishing town that flourished from the first century B.C. to sixth century A.D., Capernaum was the home of Matthew and the center of Jesus' ministry. Jesus taught in the town's synagogue and healed a centurion's servant. Excavators have unearthed a house believed to be where Peter lived and which possibly contains the room in which his mother-in-law was healed by Christ.

DAMASCUS. The capital of Syria, Damascus is an ancient oasis and important trade center. On the road to this city, Paul met the risen Christ.

EMMAUS. This settlement, which no longer exists, was located about ten miles west of Jerusalem. On the road to Emmaus, the risen Christ appeared to two of His disciples.

GADARA. East of the Jordan River and seven miles south of the Sea of Galilee, Gadara was home to both Jairus and the woman with the issue of blood. Gadara was a Greek city which, after the death of Herod, joined nine other cities to form the loose confederation called the Decapolis. These cities were self-governed and retained their Hellenistic culture.

JERICHO. A fertile oasis in the desert and the lowest town on earth, this community has survived for thousands of years. In the days of Herod, who built a winter home in Jericho, the city was full of orchards, gardens, and villas for the wealthy. Outside Jericho, Jesus met Zacchaeus, the rich tax collector in the tree, and Bartimaeus, the blind man.

JERUSALEM. Jesus healed ten lepers outside this city, which was the home of Nicodemus and the rich young ruler as well as Pilate, the high priest Caiaphas, the Sanhedrin, the Sadducees, and the Pharisees. The ruins called the Palatial Mansion, unearthed in Jerusalem, contain colorful mosaics, handpainted frescoes, and large steam baths, a testimony to the beautiful homes once owned by wealthy Jerusalem citizens like the rich young ruler.

JORDAN RIVER. The location of Christ's baptism by John the Baptist.

MAGDALA. A village on the western edge of the Sea of Galilee, Magdala was the home of Mary Magdalene and is the present-day el-Mejdel.

MOUNT OF OLIVES. This ridge, east of Jerusalem and just over the Kidron Valley, was where Jesus went to pray after the Passover supper and where He was arrested.

NAZARETH. The hometown of Jesus, Nazareth still lies about ninety miles north of Jerusalem, cradled in a valley above the Sea of Galilee.

SEA OF GALILEE. Jesus' ministry was primarily in the region surrounding this large lake in the northern part of Israel. Here He called His first disciples, calmed the storm, and walked on water. Through the centuries, the Sea of Galilee has also been called the Sea of Chinnereth, the Sea of Tiberias, and the Sea of Gennesaret.

SYCHAR. A town in Samaria near Jacob's well where Jesus met the Samaritan woman.

Index

Italicized page numbers refer to illustrations.

Photography Credits

Cover: Modern-day Israel, H. Armstrong Roberts. **Page 4–5:** World Image/FPG International. **9:** Ideals Publications Inc. **11:** Ideals Publications Inc. **12:** Superstock. **13:** top photo, Superstock; middle photo, Erich Lessing/Art Resource, NY; bottom photo, Superstock. **17:** Ideals Publications Inc. **31:** Ideals Publications Inc. **32–33:** Superstock. **34–35:** Superstock. **37:** FPG International. **39:** Superstock. **43:** Superstock. **44–45:** Superstock. **46:** Superstock. **47:** top right photo, Richard Nowitz/FPG International; bottom left photo, Erich Lessing/Art Resource, NY. 48–49: Superstock. **51:** Louis Goldman/FPG International. **54:** Superstock. **56:** Superstock. **58–59:** Superstock. **60–61:** Dave Bartruff/FPG International. **63:** Ideals Publications Inc. **65:** Dave Bartruff/FPG International. **68:** S. Kanna/FPG International. **72:** Superstock. **77:** Superstock. **78:** Ideals Publications Inc. **80:** Christian Michaels/FPG International. **81:** top left photo, Erich Lessing/Art Resource, NY; bottom right photo, Superstock. **83:** Ideals Publica-

tions Inc. **85:** Ideals Publications Inc. **88–89:** FPG International. **90–91:** Superstock. **95:** Superstock. **96:** lower left photo, FPG International; upper right photo, Erich Lessing/Art Resource, NY. **97:** FPG International. **99:** FPG International. **100:** Superstock. **102–103:** Art Resource, NY. **106–107:** Superstock. **109:** Superstock. **115:** National Museum of American Art, Washington, D.C./Art Resource, NY. **117:** Ideals Publications Inc. **118:** Ideals Publications Inc. **121:** Ideals Publications Inc. **123:** Superstock. **124:** Richard Nowitz/FPG International. **126:** Superstock. **127:** top left photo, Superstock; bottom right photo: Ulf Sjostedt/FPG International. **128–129:** Superstock. **131:** Superstock. **132:** Superstock. **134–135:** Richard Nowitz/FPG International. **137:** Superstock. **140:** Superstock. **144:** Superstock. **147:** Ideals Publications Inc. **150–151:** Superstock. **152:** Roy King/Superstock. **153:** Superstock. **154:** Ideals Publications Inc. **156–157:** Christian Michaels/FPG International.